THIS BOOK BELONGS TO:

CHRISTMAS 2003

Christmas
with Southern Living
2003

Christmas
with Southern Living
2003

Edited by Rebecca Brennan and Julie Gunter

Oxmoor
House.

©2003 by Oxmoor House, Inc.
Book Division of Southern Progress Corporation
P. O. Box 2463, Birmingham, Alabama 35201

Southern Living® is a federally registered trademark belonging to
Southern Living, Inc.

ISBN: 0-8487-2735-5
ISSN: 0747-7791
Printed in the United States of America
First Printing 2003

Editor-in-Chief: Nancy Fitzpatrick Wyatt
Executive Editor: Susan Carlisle Payne
Art Director: Cynthia Rose Cooper
Copy Chief: Catherine Ritter Scholl

Christmas with Southern Living® 2003

Editor: Rebecca Brennan
Foods Editor: Julie Gunter
Associate Editor: Susan Ray
Editorial Assistant: McCharen Pratt
Senior Photographer: Jim Bathie
Senior Photo Stylist: Kay E. Clarke
Photo Stylist: Ashley Wyatt
Illustrator: Kelly Davis
Director, Test Kitchens: Elizabeth Tyler Luckett
Assistant Director, Test Kitchens: Julie Christopher
Recipe Editor: Gayle Hays Sadler
Test Kitchens Staff: Kristi Carter, Jennifer A. Cofield, Nicole Faber,
    Ana Price Kelly, Kathleen Royal Phillips, Jan A. Smith, Elise Weis,
    Kelley Self Wilton
Publishing Systems Administrator: Rick Tucker
Director, Production and Distribution: Phillip Lee
Books Production Manager: Theresa L. Beste
Production Assistant: Faye Porter Bonner

Contributors
Designer: Nancy Johnson
Editorial: Lauren Caswell Brooks, Leah Marlett
Copy Editor: Adrienne Short Davis
Photographer: Ralph Anderson
Photo Stylist: Connie Formby
Interns: Sallie Cathey, Traci Higgins, Sarah Miller, Terri Laschober

Front cover: Holiday Lane Cake, page 151
Back cover, clockwise from top left: Southern Snowman, pages 32–33;
Spinach- and Herb-Stuffed Turkey Roll, pages 140–141; Let It Snow, pages
20–21; Streusel-Sour Cream Coffee Cake, pages 148–149
Back flap: Cream Cheese Pound Cake, page 128

To order additional publications, call 1-800-765-6400.

For more books to enrich your life, visit **oxmoorhouse.com**

CONTENTS

GIFTS & WRAPPINGS • 92

HOLIDAY RECIPES • 124

SEASONAL
STYLE

Decorating is a delight during this season of the year.
These pages offer inspiration for decking your halls with
fragrance, beauty, and welcoming charm.

CHRISTMAS DECORATIONS

Ribbons, fruits, flowers, and evergreens are the festive ingredients that make the rooms showcased on these pages sparkle. Natural materials, most of which can be found in backyards throughout the South, provide a grand (and thrifty!) starting point.

▲ GREETINGS OF GREENERY

A banister and a door frame draped with Fraser fir and brightened by small bundles of fruit welcome guests into the foyer. A gracious Christmas tree placed by a large front window can be viewed from the entrance.

A FRESH WELCOME ▶

Diminutive mums and rosy pepperberries add texture and color to a ring of greens, while the charming combination adorns an angel below. Winter's frigid temperatures and a daily misting will help these naturals last longer.

◀ HANGING GREENS

Opportunities abound for sweeping displays of lavish greenery. Silver and gold grapevine balls dress up the garland around the stately mirror, while bundles of greenery, feathers, and berries dot the banister. Bouquets of evergreens and berries tucked into wicker cones elegantly suspended from the lantern serve as the room's centerpiece.

▲ ALL THROUGH THE HOUSE

Wreaths aren't just for the front door—they can bring Christmas cheer to just about any room. Here, a circle of bay leaves and pepperberries hanging on the front of a mirror makes a splash in a guest bath. A pair of grapevine trees covered with pepperberries and embellished with bay leaves complements the wreath.

JOLLY GREEN CENTERPIECE ▼

Crystal cake plates piled with grapes, kiwifruit, limes, artichokes, and pears join with lime green candles and fabric for a dazzling centerpiece. A chandelier trimmed with ornaments continues the decoration to the ceiling.

FRUIT LOOPED ▶

Swags of tangerines strung on florist wire and punctuated by bundles of pineapple, apples, pears, and kumquats add a playful touch to a greenery garland. An arrangement of greens, fruit, candles, and flowers decorates the tabletop.

ROSE MERRY

A twist on traditional mistletoe, red rose kissing balls dance above petite bouquets of roses blooming from silver cups and a pair of rose-covered topiaries. Small sprigs of Fraser fir and boxwood give the arrangement a colorful Christmas combination. These three elegant spheres were made by inserting cut roses into a water-soaked florist foam ball. The topiaries were created by gluing rose petals onto craft-foam tree forms.

▲ MANTEL MAGIC

Mantel arrangements can be the focal point for your holiday decorating whether simple or complex. Consider using the mantel to display a collection such as these Christmas carolers whose colors and mood blend beautifully with the painting already in place above the mantel. Magnolia, abundant in gardens in much of the South, mixed with Fraser fir cut from the base of the Christmas tree enlivens the setting.

ABUNDANTLY APPEALING ▶

Create an elaborate decoration by piling on the greenery and natural materials. Fraser fir and magnolia are wired together, draped across the mantel, and wrapped with ribbon for a lush look. Greenery and berries pressed into water-soaked florist foam overflow from a container centered on the mantel. Before beginning, condition the greens by trimming the ends and letting them soak overnight—that will help them stay fresh longer.

LET IT SNOW ▶

Snowflakes drifting across the mantel bring a white Christmas indoors. The arrangement also includes two charming snowmen, four patchwork stockings, greens, candles, and berries. Each snowman is created by piercing three water-soaked florist foam spheres with a 12-inch florist stick. The cut stems of carnations are inserted into the spheres until the balls are completely covered. Eyes and buttons made of red carnations, arms of berries, and a mouth and hair of greens give each snowman personality.

▲ CHEERFUL CHAIR

Packages needn't be placed just under the tree—use them to cheer up any spot of the house. Here, a few sit on a chair decorated with a small snowflake ornament and a Christmas pillow. A halo of winter-white berries tied onto one of the gifts makes a divine package topper.

▲ CRANBERRY CREATIONS

Glass jars and pedestals filled with cranberries and topped with white roses and candles make a refreshing seasonal vignette. Red-and-white accessories give any arrangement instant holiday pizzazz.

SENSATIONAL SETTING ▶

Candles illuminate cups and vases holding red roses, anemones, white wax flowers, ranunculus, berries, and greens. An inverted grapevine-and-berry tree serves as a vase above the grouping.

RED, WHITE, AND GREENS

The combination of greenery, ornaments, and red berries brings the holidays into an old-fashioned cupboard. Pieces of silverware incorporated into the garland convey a playful, culinary feel.

FRESH-AIR CELEBRATION

The South's occasional mild winter afternoons create a chance for a pleasant outdoor gathering. Dress up plain wooden chairs by tying moss-wrapped wire ribbon into bows and embellishing them with berries and leaves. The moss ribbon is repeated in the centerpiece along with magnolia and berries. If it happens to be too cold to entertain outdoors, guests will enjoy viewing the charming tablesetting from inside.

OUTDOOR ELEGANCE

Nothing says Christmas like the brisk scent of fresh evergreens. Fortunately, they're amazingly abundant and inexpensive. We gathered ideas here for using greenery in lots of decorative ways—some traditional, some whimsical, all simple to do. You're sure to find something just right for your home.

▲ VICTORIAN CHARM

There's a hint of Charles Dickens's England in these stately lanterns, but the natural materials are decidedly American South. To achieve this look, wire clippings into small bundles, then wire the bundles to the lamppost. Finish with a big red bow to complement the deep greens of the pine, cedar, holly, and magnolia.

MIX WELL ▶

This entry decoration is not fussy, yet it's dramatic enough to make an impression. On the front door wreath the only embellishment is a red plaid bow. Iron candleholders, though simple, blend nicely with the wreath. The greenery and ribbons are wired to the candleholders. Place fresh flower stems in florist water picks to keep blooms fresh.

EVERGREEN ESSENTIALS

Your own backyard is probably the best source for greenery and berries for your evergreen arrangements. If you're short on supplies, perhaps a generous neighbor will give you clipping privileges.

Any number of trees and shrubs in your yard are perfect for holiday decorations. Holly, cedar, nandina, aucuba, pine, cedar, and boxwood are all good choices. Select a variety of shades of green for maximum impact.

Florist foam (available at crafts and florist shops) comes in many different shapes and sizes. Soak florist foam in water before inserting flower or greenery stems. The foam helps keep materials fresh and gives you better control when creating your decorations.

Florist picks, wire, and tape (available at crafts and florist shops) make working with greenery much easier. Use picks to secure fruit to wreaths and garlands. Use chicken wire to wrap large blocks of florist foam. It helps hold the greenery and foam together.

MORE IS MERRIER

Repetition makes this door decoration charming. Where one wreath is
lovely, four multiplies the welcoming effect. Jumbo jingle bells threaded
onto the ribbon streamers sound a gentle chime every time the door opens.

◀ ALFRESCO ENTERTAINING

Take advantage of the South's mild winter days with an open-air feast. With the great outdoors as your setting, you need only minimal table decorations—a few potted evergreens and some pinecones scattered down the center of the table.

▲ SURPRISINGLY SIMPLE STYLE

A metal cone wired to the lamppost holds a sprightly bouquet of winter greens. Many types of containers can be used in this fashion, such as baskets, wire-mesh cones, and small wall buckets.

Depending on the weather, the clippings should stay fresh-looking for ten days to two weeks. To ensure maximum freshness, set cut stems in a bucket of tepid water overnight before creating the arrangement; then arrange stems in the container, as desired.

◀ SOUTHERN SNOWMAN

Who needs a white Christmas to be jolly? This snowman certainly proves otherwise. Three twig or grapevine wreaths in graduated sizes form the snowman's body. A snappy hat, scarf, and boots outfit him. The hat pictured is made from sheet metal that has been spray painted black. Another option for the hat is a large coffee can affixed to a semicircle of wood or particleboard, and then painted black.

▲ THE GREAT OUTDOORS

Reminiscent of a wintry fairyland forest, this window box is a fine example of outdoor embellishments that span the season. The wreath hanging in the window gives a nod to Christmastime for an overall effect that is understated yet cozy and inviting.

▲ NATURAL BEAUTY

A vast wall basket holds an abundance of winter berries and greenery. Ivy and nandina berries spill over the sides, setting a casual mood. Arranging the clippings in florist foam inside the basket will keep the display fresh longer.

MAILBOX TIDINGS ▶

Greenery and berry clippings will look fresh outside for ten days to two weeks thanks to December's crisp, cool days, so it's not absolutely necessary to use florist foam to keep arrangements fresh. This makes it much easier to create outdoor decorations for the mailbox. Here, bunches of stems are wired together and then wired to the mailbox post. The pineapple sits on a small square of wood on the mailbox to hold it steady.

◀ SWEET-SMELLING DESIGN

On a garden wall, pots of fragrant paperwhites sit on an iron shelf. Pine and cedar branches lined along the shelf easily hide the plants' plastic containers.

GRAND IMPACT

These evergreen arrangements may look hard to do, but they're really very simple. Begin by clipping a variety of berry and greenery stems. To make the greenery stronger and last longer, place the freshly cut stems in a bucket of water overnight. While clipping, don't forget to look for bare branches and dried materials, such as seed pods, that will offer interesting texture and dimension.

For your arrangement, fill a container with moistened florist foam and position the branches by sticking them into the foam. Start with the taller branches first, then fill in with shorter ones.

Carefully water the florist foam if it becomes dry. The greenery will last up to two weeks—so you'll have a fresh and fragrant decoration throughout the holidays.

TREASURED TRIMMINGS

*Search flea markets, antique stores, and even your own attic for holiday decorations
that stand the test of time. Use a little bit of Christmas creativity to make
these classic favorites part of your annual embellishments.*

▲ BLOCK PARTY

Have some fun decorating with antique (or just vintage-looking) toys, such as these blocks which are styled with greens, candy, and tiny Santas.

CHARMING CIRCLES ▶

Tea lights wrapped with remnants of old-fashioned trim glow beneath a classic Santa and Christmas tree. Use brightly colored ribbon for a more updated look.

CELESTIAL SCENE

Angels grouped with greens, berries, ornaments, and candles take on a special meaning this time of year. Use Christmassy embellishments to accentuate any grouping of everyday collectibles.

▲ PEWTER PERFECT

Pewter, which dates back to 1500 B.C., becomes a classic combination when mixed with bright ornaments and candy. Grouping similar items creates more impact.

◀ DECKED WITH DISHES

Don't relegate Christmas china to the cupboard, display it on tabletops paired with naturals, ornaments, and ribbon. Here, the ribbons holding the ornaments are taped to the backs of the plates.

AT YOUR SERVICE

Antique trays and plates in a combination of colors, sizes, and shapes provide a nostalgic backdrop for greens, berries, and a host of angels.

TIPS FOR TRAY DISPLAYS

Trays quickly bring character to bookshelves, walls, and tabletops. With the addition of a few seasonal elements, they form the foundation for charming holiday displays.

• Organize a tabletop grouping of small treasures. Place an ornamental tray on a table, and fill the tray with Christmas ornaments, candles, and greenery.

• Feature a favorite holiday figurine or decorative piece by displaying it in front of a tall tray that's a contrasting color; or lean the tray against a wall and place a container of berries, pinecones, or flowers in front of it.

• Place a tray in the center of the dining table, and add a tall plant (such as an amaryllis or pot of paperwhites). Surround the plant with small pots of ferns or ivy. Cluster pieces of fruit, greenery, pinecones, or berries on the tray for more color.

• Collect trays in holiday colors to use instead of place mats.

PITCHER-PERFECT IDEAS

Festive decorations are right at your fingertips when you use favorite everyday pitchers and fill them with holiday blooms.

STRENGTH IN NUMBERS ▲

Lots of small pitchers positioned on and around stacked cake stands add up to a striking centerpiece. Gold ribbons and ornaments offer a warm contrast to the white tulips and ranunculus that pour over the pitchers.

OLD WORLD SIMPLICITY ▶

A transferware pitcher, bowl, and platter make a handsome container for a sideboard arrangement. The bowl and pitcher sit atop blocks of florist foam. Roses, hydrangea blooms, and berries fill the pitcher and the platter. Hydrangea blooms and berries form a fluffy skirt at the base of the pitcher.

◀ A ZESTY SCHEME

Choose a color theme for your decoration like this lively green arrangement. Pitchers in varying shades of green are complemented by green roses, mums, and apple berries. For greater impact, set the grouping in front of a mirror.

ONE CLASSIC, 4 WAYS

With their flashy foil wrappings, poinsettias often can be difficult to display with other holiday decorations. Take them out of their traditional containers to create festive arrangements that will adorn your home with classic Christmas charm.

▲ EASY IMPACT

Brilliant blooms of small red poinsettias surround an ivy topiary for a rich combination of red and green. A full green bow gives holiday flair. (Ivy topiaries are available at florist and home improvement stores.)

CLASSIC STYLE ▶

Bright red berries and an abundance of greenery underscore pale pink poinsettias nestled in an outdoor urn. If temperatures fall below 50°, lift out the poinsettia pots and store them in an enclosed area.

POINSETTIA POINTERS

If one plant symbolizes Christmas, it's the poinsettia. These tips offer suggestions for decorating with and caring for this seasonal favorite.

• To select a plant guaranteed to last, make sure the tiny yellow flowers at the center of the poinsettia are surrounded by fully-colored bracts (the colored leaves we usually refer to as the flower or bloom of the poinsettia). If you see any green there, move on to another plant.

• Poinsettias can't tolerate temperatures below 50°, so protect your plant from the cold by asking the garden center to sleeve it with cellophane. Remove the sleeve as soon as you get the plant home.

• Place a large poinsettia in a basket (or purchase one already in a basket). When your fireplace is not in use, place the plant just inside the opening. In a very small or particularly dark fireplace, use white poinsettias to make the space appear large and bright.

• Poinsettias make terrific long-lasting cut flowers if you sear the stem. Immediately after cutting, run the stem over a flame to seal it. This prevents the sticky white sap from draining out of the cut. Place the flowers in a water-filled vase or moistened florist foam.

• If your plant loses a branch on the way home, make a fresh cut in the stem, and sear it; then put the flowers in a vase or incorporate them in another arrangement.

◀ EYE-CATCHING COLOR

A handsome container and an imaginative combination of similarly-sized plants help showcase poinsettia's simplicity and elegance. Paired with vivid purple African violets, pink bracts take on a festive glow. Fern fronds and other greenery tucked in near the opening of the stone birdbath soften its hard edges.

FRESH ACCENT ▶

Creamy poinsettias—an unexpected embellishment on this holiday wreath—stand out in appealing contrast to the deep colors of the greenery wreath. Insert the poinsettia stems in water picks to keep them fresh.

10-MINUTE DECORATING

Christmas displays needn't be complicated to make an impact. Among the season's lavish arrangements, sometimes the simple touches bring the greatest pleasure.

▲ WARM REFLECTIONS

A mirror can have a strong decorative impact in areas other than the wall. Here, the light from a grouping of candles is reflected among the greenery arranged on a round mirror.

IT'S A WRAP ▶

Bunches of oranges, lemons, and limes become cheery pomanders when studded with cloves and wrapped with colorful tulle and ribbon.

▲ RUSTIC CHARM

This log candelabrum is made by drilling three holes equal to the diameter of the candles along the center top of the log. Ribbons tied around the log provide a punch of color and complement the red candles. To prevent a fire hazard, do not let the tapers burn down to the log.

A LITTLE LIGHT ▶

Short ribbon remnants leftover from holiday wrappings look elegant wrapped around a pillar candle and embell-ished with winter berries. Be sure to never leave burning candles unattended.

CREATIVE PAPERS

It takes just a few minutes to turn plain pillars into stunning decorations.
For each candle, cut a length of handmade paper or decorative tissue to fit
around the candle. Wrap the paper around the candle, overlapping the ends,
and use double-stick tape to hold the paper in place.

FESTIVE FRUIT

Bright-colored ribbons dangle lemons, limes, and oranges from the window. Florist wire pressed through the fruits secures them to the ribbons. This decoration will last at least a week, depending on the freshness of the fruit. See page 172 for directions and how-to photographs.

▲ GARLAND OF GREETINGS

Use holiday cards to create a one-of-a-kind decoration for the mantel. Simply drape a wide length of ribbon from side to side and tie on your favorite cards using smaller lengths of ribbon.

◀ STAR LIGHT, STAR BRIGHT

No room to decorate? Try looking up. Here, clusters of berries are wired to the chandelier, while sparkling star ornaments suspend from strips of ribbons.

FRUIT AND BERRY ACCENTS ▶

Add a cheerful embellishment to a basic ivy topiary by tucking bright berries and pears around the base. Ivy topiaries can be found at florist shops, floral departments of grocery stores, and home improvement centers.

ENTERTAINING

We set the stage for carefree entertaining with a pair of casual make-ahead buffets and some table settings worth talking about.

SPLASHY CENTERPIECE

Choose an impressive architectural piece, such as this urn, for displaying a centerpiece. Place a large bowl filled with water-soaked florist foam in the urn; secure the foam with florist tape. Tuck Fraser fir clippings (gathered from a Christmas tree lot or your own tree) around the base. Stick branches of holly berries into the foam in the center of the arrangement; fill in with tulips (available at florists and grocery stores) and more berries.

SUPPER CLUB
Christmas Party

*Pamper your friends with this gourmet fare,
the glow of candles, and good conversation.
It's a serve-yourself buffet, so the hosts
can have fun, too.*

BUFFET FOR 16

Grapefruit Margaritas
Cran-Ginger Spritzers
Smoky Nuts   Cranberry Brie

Beef Tenderloin with Shallot Sauce
Marinated Mushrooms with Honey and Sage
Caramelized Onion Bread Pudding
Broccoli with Pancetta and Lemon
Molten Chocolate Cakes
Wine (see page 67)   Coffee

MAKE-AHEAD PARTY PLAN

Want to host a relaxing party? Follow the plan below, and enjoy the fun as much as your guests.

1 WEEK AHEAD:
- *Make grocery list. Shop for nonperishables.*

2 OR 3 DAYS AHEAD:
- *Take inventory of china, serving dishes, and utensils. Gather whatever pieces you'll need. Polish silver.*
- *Shop for perishables.*
- *Plan centerpiece and other table decorations.*
- *Prepare Smoky Nuts, and store in airtight container.*

1 DAY AHEAD:
- *Prepare Grapefruit Margaritas and freeze.*
- *Toast bread for bread pudding. Store in a large zip-top bag.*
- *Caramelize onions; refrigerate overnight.*
- *Blanch broccoli, if desired (first step in recipe). Refrigerate in a large zip-top bag.*

MORNING OF PARTY:
- *Prepare and chill chocolate cake batter in muffin cups.*
- *Prepare Cranberry Brie, but don't heat. Store in refrigerator.*
- *Prepare dressing for marinated mushrooms.*
- *Chill cranberry-apple juice drink and ginger ale for spritzers.*

2½ HOURS BEFORE THE MEAL:
- *First prepare and bake bread pudding. Let stand at room temperature.*
- *Then prepare and bake tenderloin with shallot sauce.*

1 HOUR BEFORE THE MEAL:
- *Finish preparing Broccoli with Pancetta and Lemon.*
- *Marinate mushrooms in dressing for at least 30 minutes.*

JUST BEFORE SERVING:
- *Heat Cranberry Brie in microwave.*
- *Set out beverages. No need to thaw margaritas.*
- *Reheat bread pudding, uncovered, at 350° for 10 minutes.*

JUST AFTER DINNER:
- *Bake chocolate cakes. Brew coffee.*
- *Set out coffee and cakes for guests to serve themselves.*

Cranberry Brie, page 65

AN ICY INKLING

Here's a frosty idea for your beverage bar. Line a metal tub with a plastic bag; fill with ice. Add pitchers of Grapefruit Margaritas. Nestle some glassware into ice, too. Add sprigs of greenery around edge of tub.

ANYTHING GOES WITH GLASSWARE

Serve beverages in whatever shaped glassware you have. Mix and match glassware to keep it casual. We broke the rules to serve margaritas in trendy martini glasses. You can, too.

Grapefruit Margaritas, page 64

Smoky Nuts, page 64

GRAPEFRUIT MARGARITAS

Ruby red grapefruit juice casts a pretty hue over this margarita. Buy bottled juice so you can sip the frosty refresher year-round. Make and freeze it ahead to get slushy results and save time right before your party.

1   (6-ounce) container frozen limeade concentrate
⅔   cup ruby red grapefruit juice
⅔   cup white tequila
¼   cup orange liqueur (we tested with Triple Sec)

Combine all ingredients in an electric blender, adding ice to 3½ cup level. Process just until ice is finely crushed. Pour into a pitcher and serve immediately, or cover and freeze. Yield: 3½ cups.

Note: *For the freshest flavor, squeeze your own grapefruit juice. Try freezing juice in ice cube trays; add frozen cubes to blender.*

Make Ahead: *If you want slushy margaritas for a crowd, make several batches in advance and freeze until ready to serve. There's no need to thaw them; just stir and serve.*

▲ **CRAN-GINGER SPRITZERS** are a glittering nonalcoholic drink option for the evening. Chill bottles of cranberry-apple juice drink and ginger ale. To serve, pour equal amounts of each into a pitcher or glasses.

SMOKY NUTS

Pecans and almonds are glazed in a sweet, smoky blend of honey and chipotle peppers. Find chipotle peppers on the Mexican food aisle.

¼   cup honey
2   tablespoons sugar
2   tablespoons chipotle peppers with 1 teaspoon pepper
     liquid, pureed
1½   cups pecan halves
1½   cups whole almonds
Salt

Combine first 3 ingredients in a medium saucepan. Cook over medium heat until sugar dissolves, stirring often. Stir in nuts.

Spread coated nuts in a single layer in a lightly greased 15" x 10" jellyroll pan. Bake at 300° for 20 minutes. Stir, and bake 10 to 15 more minutes. Spread warm nuts onto aluminum foil or parchment paper; separate nuts with a fork. Lightly sprinkle with salt. Cool before serving. Store nuts between layers of parchment paper or wax paper in an airtight container up to 3 days. Yield: 3½ cups.

Note: *You can use 3 cups of any one type of nut for this recipe, if desired.*

CRANBERRY BRIE Make Ahead • Quick & Easy

A wheel of buttery Brie is crowned with a glistening mix of cranberries, pecans, brown sugar, and honey.

1   (8") round Brie (about 2 pounds; or see box at right)
¾   cup dried cranberries or sweetened dried cranberries
¾   cup finely chopped pecans
3   tablespoons light brown sugar
¼   cup honey

Trim rind from top of Brie, leaving a ½" border. Place Brie on a microwave-safe plate.

Combine cranberries, pecans, and sugar; sprinkle over Brie. Drizzle with honey. Cover and chill until ready to heat.

Microwave at HIGH 1½ to 2 minutes or just until cheese is softened. Serve with crackers and pear slices. Yield: 16 appetizer servings.

FOR ENTERTAINING

If you can't find a 2-pound wheel of Brie, buy 4 (8-ounce) rounds of Brie. Divide the topping evenly among the 4 rounds and microwave, 2 at a time, at HIGH 1½ minutes. For an interesting presentation, stack the Brie on a serving tray.

BEEF TENDERLOIN WITH SHALLOT SAUCE

Marsala wine and charred shallots impart their essence to this tenderloin's deep brown sauce, creating a depth of flavor that's rich and smoky.

1   pound shallots, peeled and halved lengthwise
2   tablespoons olive oil
¾   teaspoon salt
½   teaspoon pepper
1   tablespoon salt
1½   teaspoons onion powder
1½   teaspoons garlic powder
1½   teaspoons pepper
1½   teaspoons chopped fresh or ½ teaspoon dried thyme
1   (6-pound) beef tenderloin, trimmed
¼   cup olive oil
3   cups beef broth
1   cup dry Marsala wine
2   tablespoons all-purpose flour
3   tablespoons water
3   tablespoons butter or margarine
¼   teaspoon pepper
Garnish: fresh thyme

Toss shallots and 2 tablespoons oil in a bowl; stir in ¾ teaspoon salt and ½ teaspoon pepper. Set aside.

Stir together 1 tablespoon salt and next 4 ingredients. Rub tenderloin with ¼ cup olive oil; sprinkle seasonings over top and sides of tenderloin, pressing gently with fingers. Place tenderloin in a large greased roasting pan; arrange shallots around tenderloin. Bake, uncovered, at 500° for 25 minutes. Reduce oven temperature to 375°, and bake 15 to 20 minutes or until meat thermometer inserted into thickest part of roast registers 145° (medium-rare) or 160° (medium).

Meanwhile, stir together beef broth and Marsala in a large skillet. Bring to a boil; boil 6 to 8 minutes or until liquid is reduced to 2 cups.

Remove tenderloin to a serving platter and cover with aluminum foil; reserve shallots and drippings in pan. Add broth reduction to pan, and place over medium heat on cooktop, stirring to loosen particles from bottom of pan.

Whisk together flour and water until smooth; stir into sauce in roasting pan. Cook over medium heat, stirring constantly, until slightly thickened. Add butter, stirring just until melted. Stir in ¼ teaspoon pepper. Thinly slice roast, and serve with sauce. Garnish, if desired. Yield: 16 servings.

MARINATED MUSHROOMS WITH HONEY AND SAGE   _{Make Ahead}

Earthy mushrooms are marinated in a fusion of fresh sage, honey, and walnut oil.

2   shallots, finely chopped
2   garlic cloves, minced
½   cup walnut oil
¼   cup white wine vinegar
¼   cup honey
¼   cup loosely packed fresh sage leaves, chopped
1   teaspoon salt
½   teaspoon freshly ground pepper
6   (8-ounce) packages small fresh mushrooms
Garnish: fresh sage

Whisk together first 8 ingredients in a large bowl; add mushrooms. Let stand at least 30 minutes, stirring occasionally. Serve at room temperature with a slotted spoon. Garnish, if desired. Yield: 8 cups.

FOR ENTERTAINING

HIGH-STYLE 'SHROOMS
Dress up this marinated mushroom salad by serving it in a footed dish or trifle bowl.

WINE & DINE
We recommend any of these wines with dinner: Morgan Monterey Syrah, Chateau Souverain Dry Creek Zinfandel, or Bleasdale Langhorne Creek Shiraz-Cabernet.

Caramelized Onion Bread Pudding

CARAMELIZED ONION BREAD PUDDING

Make Ahead

Fresh rosemary and caramelized onions are the stars of this savory bread pudding.

1   (1-pound) loaf country bread, cut into 1" cubes
½   cup butter or margarine
4   large onions, sliced
10 large eggs, lightly beaten
2   quarts half-and-half
¼   cup chopped fresh rosemary
1   tablespoon salt
½   teaspoon freshly ground pepper

Place bread cubes in a large roasting pan. Bake at 250° for 30 minutes, tossing occasionally. Turn oven off, and let bread stand in oven 1 to 1½ hours or until dried. (Cover roasting pan with foil and leave bread in oven overnight, if desired.)

Melt butter in a large skillet over high heat. Add onion, and cook 15 minutes, stirring occasionally. Reduce heat to medium, and cook, stirring often, 15 to 20 minutes or until onion is caramelized. Remove from heat. Refrigerate overnight, if desired.

Toss bread and caramelized onion together in pan.

Whisk together eggs, half-and-half, rosemary, salt, and pepper in a large bowl; pour over bread and onion in pan, and stir gently. Let stand at room temperature at least 1 hour, stirring occasionally to coat bread.

Bake, uncovered, at 375° for 1 to 1¼ hours or until firm and lightly browned. Let stand 10 minutes before serving. Yield: 16 servings.

BROCCOLI WITH PANCETTA AND LEMON

Make Ahead

Pancetta is an Italian bacon that is cured and spiced, but not smoked. The bacon, garlic, and lemon make plain broccoli great.

4   (12-ounce) packages broccoli florets
6   tablespoons butter or margarine, divided
¼   pound pancetta, chopped
4   garlic cloves, minced
2   tablespoons grated lemon zest
1   teaspoon salt

Bring several quarts of water to a boil in a large Dutch oven. Add broccoli florets, and simmer 2 minutes or until crisp-tender. (Cook in batches, if necessary.) Drain and plunge broccoli into a bowl of ice water to stop cooking process. Drain and pat dry.

Melt 3 tablespoons butter in a large skillet over medium-high heat. Add half of pancetta and half of garlic; sauté 2 to 3 minutes or until lightly browned. Add half of broccoli florets, and sauté 2 to 3 minutes until thoroughly heated. Add 1 tablespoon lemon zest and ½ teaspoon salt; toss well. Transfer to a large bowl; cover and keep warm. Repeat procedure with remaining 3 tablespoons butter and remaining half of ingredients. Serve warm or at room temperature. Yield: 16 servings.

Make Ahead: *Cook broccoli and pat dry a day ahead; store in zip-top plastic bags in refrigerator.*

Note: *Find pancetta in the deli meat department of large supermarkets. Regular bacon makes a fine substitute in this recipe.*

Broccoli with Pancetta and Lemon

10 PARTY POINTERS

1 Plan your menu and review recipes a week or two before party time. Make a general grocery list. Go ahead and shop for specialty items such as wine, crackers, and cheeses.

2 Organize in advance. Plan your table settings, serving dishes, and decorations. Borrow or buy if needed.

3 Serve appetizers in the kitchen; that's where guests tend to gather initially.

4 Set up a beverage station near the kitchen so it will be convenient to replenish ice, frozen drinks, and glassware.

5 Open wine before guests arrive. Briefly chill white wine. Prepare coffee for brewing, but wait until dinner plates are cleared to brew it. Have a sugar substitute on hand.

6 Make it easy on yourself. Serve as many room temperature dishes as possible. Choose recipes you can prepare ahead.

7 Have an empty dishwasher when the evening begins. Check your supply of kitchen garbage bags.

8 Use different rooms for different courses. Serve one course outside if weather permits.

9 Gather a good stack of CDs for the evening and place them near CD player. Ask your spouse or a close friend to be in charge of music.

10 Indulge your guests. There's no such thing as too many sweets. If you offer one decadent homemade dessert, have another simple option, such as storebought specialty cookies or dessert cheese and nuts.

Molten Chocolate Cakes

MOLTEN CHOCOLATE CAKES Make Ahead

These yummy little cakes ooze soft chocolate from the center when you spoon into them.

2 tablespoons butter, melted
2 tablespoons unsweetened cocoa
¾ cup butter, cut into pieces
3 (4-ounce) bars premium semisweet chocolate, broken into chunks (we tested with Ghirardelli)
½ cup whipping cream
1¼ cups egg substitute (see Note)
¾ cup sugar
⅔ cup all-purpose flour
Powdered sugar

Brush 16 muffin pans with 2 tablespoons melted butter. Sprinkle evenly with cocoa, shaking out excess. Place in refrigerator to firm butter.

Place ¾ cup butter and chocolate in a large heavy saucepan. Cook over low heat, stirring often, until butter and chocolate melt. Slowly whisk in cream; set aside.

Combine egg substitute and sugar in a large mixing bowl. Beat at medium speed with an electric mixer 5 to 7 minutes or until slightly thickened; add chocolate cream and flour, beating until blended. Pour batter into muffin cups, filling to within ¼" from tops. Cover and chill at least 1 hour or up to 24 hours.

Bake at 450° for 10 to 11 minutes or just until edges of cakes spring back when lightly touched, but centers are still soft. Let stand 3 minutes before loosening edges with a knife. Quickly invert cakes onto a baking sheet. Transfer to dessert plates using a spatula. Sprinkle with powdered sugar. Serve warm. Yield: 16 servings.

Note: *The recipe uses egg substitute instead of real eggs because the cakes aren't in the oven long enough for eggs to cook thoroughly.*

Serve this Christmas feast as a casual buffet. See page 78 for the centerpiece how-to and page 187 for general buffet tips.

ULTIMATE *Southern* CHRISTMAS DINNER

The South's best flavors shine in this holiday spread. A golden bird with giblet gravy, comfort food casseroles, and a stellar cake line up on this sumptuous buffet.

BUFFET FOR 10 TO 12

Seasoned Roast Turkey
Giblet Gravy   Cornbread-Biscuit Dressing
Green Peas and Baby Limas with Pine Nuts
Swiss-Squash Casserole
Gingersnap Sweet Potatoes
Cranberry-Kumquat Relish
Holiday Lane Cake (see page 151)
Cranberry-Lime Sherbet
Iced tea   Coffee

CHRISTMAS COUNTDOWN

*Hoping to be a more carefree Christmas host this year?
Let this layout be your guide.*

1 WEEK AHEAD:
- *Make grocery list. Shop for nonperishables.*
- *Bake Lane cake layers. Wrap and freeze.*

2 OR 3 DAYS AHEAD:
- *Take inventory of china, serving dishes, and utensils.
  Gather whatever pieces you'll need. Polish silver.*
- *Shop for perishables.*
- *Plan centerpiece and other table decorations.*
- *Prepare and freeze Cranberry-Lime Sherbet.*
- *Thaw turkey, if frozen.*
- *Prepare Cranberry-Kumquat Relish.*

1 DAY AHEAD:
- *Prepare dressing; chill overnight unbaked.*
- *Prepare sweet potato casserole filling. Chill overnight.*
- *Prepare filling for Lane cake; chill overnight. Thaw layers.*

CHRISTMAS MORNING:
- *Bake dressing. Cover and set aside.*
- *Make frosting, and assemble Lane cake.*

SEVERAL HOURS BEFORE THE MEAL:
- *Prepare and roast turkey.*
- *Simmer broth for gravy (2 hours).*
- *Prepare squash casserole; cover and chill until ready to bake.*

1 HOUR BEFORE THE MEAL:
- *Cook peas and limas. Keep in skillet to reheat at last minute.*
- *Bake squash casserole when turkey's done roasting.*
- *Microwave sweet potato filling; then prepare and
  add streusel, and bake when squash comes out of oven.*

JUST BEFORE SERVING:
- *Finish gravy.*
- *Reheat dressing.*

SEASONED ROAST TURKEY

*This gorgeous turkey is seasoned with nine spices for flavor
impact. Note that it also releases lots of delectable drippings
for some dynamite gravy.*

1	(12- to 14-pound) fresh or frozen turkey, thawed
1	tablespoon salt
2	teaspoons seasoned salt
1	teaspoon ground black pepper
1	teaspoon poultry seasoning
1	teaspoon garlic powder
1	teaspoon paprika
1	teaspoon ground red pepper
1	teaspoon dried basil
½	teaspoon ground ginger
2	tablespoons butter or margarine, softened
1	cup water

Garnishes: kumquats, fresh sage, fresh rosemary

Remove giblets and neck from turkey; reserve for making Giblet Gravy (page 76), if desired. Rinse turkey with cold water; pat dry. Place turkey, breast side up, in a greased broiler pan. Combine salt and next 8 ingredients. Using fingers, carefully loosen skin from turkey at neck area, working down to breast and thigh area. Rub about one-third of seasonings under skin. Rub skin with softened butter; rub with remaining seasonings. Tie legs together with heavy string, or tuck under flap of skin. Lift wing tips up and over back; tuck under turkey.

Add water to pan. Cover turkey with aluminum foil. Bake at 325° for 3 to 3½ hours or until a meat thermometer inserted into meaty part of thigh registers 180°, uncovering turkey after 2 hours. Transfer turkey to a serving platter, reserving pan drippings for gravy. Let turkey stand 15 minutes before carving. Garnish, if desired. Yield: 12 to 14 servings.

*Tip: If you buy a frozen bird, remember to allow about 3 days
for a 12- to 14-pound turkey to thaw in the refrigerator.*

Seasoned Roast Turkey

GIBLET GRAVY

If you often wish you had more gravy left after a holiday meal, this recipe is for you. A long-simmering broth and pan drippings contribute rich flavor to this abundant gravy that's not overly thick.

Neck and giblets reserved from turkey
4   cups water
1   celery rib with leaves, cut into pieces
1   onion, quartered
½   cup all-purpose flour
½   cup water
½   teaspoon salt
1   teaspoon pepper

Combine first 4 ingredients in a large saucepan. Bring to a boil; cover, reduce heat, and simmer 2 hours, removing liver after 20 minutes to prevent overcooking. Remove from heat. Pour broth through a wire-mesh strainer into a bowl. Remove neck meat from bone; chop, and set aside. Chop remaining giblets, and set aside.

Stir 3½ cups broth into reserved turkey drippings in broiler pan that turkey roasted in, or in a large saucepan. Bring to a boil. Combine flour and ½ cup water, stirring until smooth; gradually whisk into boiling broth. Add salt and pepper. Reduce heat to medium, and cook, whisking constantly, 5 minutes or until thickened. Stir in chopped neck meat and giblets; cook until thoroughly heated. Yield: 6½ cups.

CORNBREAD-BISCUIT DRESSING

Make Ahead

This simple Old South dressing is a no-egg recipe, so it's slightly crumbly. We liked it smothered in Giblet Gravy.

4   cups biscuit crumbs (see shortcut at right)
4   cups cornbread crumbs
6   celery ribs, chopped
1   large onion, chopped
⅓   cup butter or margarine, melted
½   cup chopped fresh parsley
1   tablespoon chopped fresh or 1 teaspoon dried sage
1   teaspoon salt
1   teaspoon pepper
2½   cups chicken or turkey broth
½   cup milk

Spread biscuit and cornbread crumbs in an ungreased pan. Bake at 300° for 15 minutes or until crumbs are toasted, stirring twice.

Sauté celery and onion in butter in a large skillet over medium-high heat until tender. Remove from heat. Combine sautéed mixture, toasted crumbs, parsley, and next 3 ingredients. Stir in broth and milk. Spoon dressing into a greased 13" x 9" pan. Bake, uncovered, at 350° for 1 hour or until browned. Yield: 10 servings.

Shortcut Solution: *Six frozen biscuits, baked, or six fast-food biscuits will give you 4 cups crumbs. We tested with Pillsbury frozen biscuits and Pioneer cornbread mix. You could also use frozen baked cornbread and warm it in the microwave oven before crumbling. Or buy cornbread from a cafeteria or deli.*

Make Ahead: *Spoon prepared dressing into pan; cover and chill overnight. Bake, uncovered, at 350° for 1 hour. Let stand at room temperature until almost serving time. Just before serving, reheat at 350° for 10 to 12 minutes.*

SECOND TIME AROUND

Want some fresh ideas for holiday leftovers? We polled the experts on staff for some tasty feedback.

• Reheat and eat dressing for breakfast, right next to those scrambled eggs and grits.

• Make a deluxe turkey sandwich using turkey slices, dressing, gravy, and cranberry sauce with a dab of mayonnaise on your favorite bread. Another turkey sandwich idea highlights turkey, salt, pepper, mayonnaise, and thinly sliced Granny Smith apple.

• Use the turkey carcass and leftover meat to make gumbo.

• Make turkey hash, and serve it over hot biscuits.

• Make a turkey pot pie using chopped turkey and refrigerated piecrusts.

• Shape leftover cold mashed potatoes into patties, and fry them in a skillet for breakfast.

• Make a pan of turkey tetrazzini. Freeze it, and pull it out when you're in the casserole mood.

• Make a sumptuous omelet with chopped turkey, cheese, sautéed onion, and green pepper.

• Use leftover dressing as a casserole topping.

• Spoon your homemade cranberry relish over vanilla ice cream; top with a sugar cookie. Or reheat sweet potato casserole (the kind with crunchy sweet topping), and enjoy it with praline ice cream as dessert.

• Package single-serving divided plates with leftovers, pop them in large zip-top freezer bags, and pass them out to relatives who live alone to take home and reheat.

• Prepare an extra plate, and take it to a friend or family member who has to work on holiday.

• Divide unbaked dressing into portions. Bake enough for the holiday meal. Package and freeze remaining portions up to 3 months. For a pseudoholiday meal at another time, heat thawed dressing at 350° for 30 minutes and roast a whole chicken at 400° for 45 minutes to go along.

• Substitute turkey for chicken in some favorite familiar entrées.

• Serve "instant replay" of the holiday feast the next day. It might just taste better because all the cooking's been done and there's not as much clean up.

CRANBERRY AND KUMQUAT CENTERPIECE

Layer glass vase or jar with fresh cranberries and kumquats. For each vase, take plantings from a 4-pack of pansies and, along with dirt and roots, tuck them into a small plastic bag. Nestle flower bag down into cranberries, hiding the bag and adding extra cranberries at top, as needed. The centerpiece will stay fresh 3 to 4 days.

ONE-OVEN CHRISTMAS

Dreaming of a double oven for Christmas? Never fear. Here are some options for single oven survival.

• *Use electric heating plates to keep made-ahead dishes warm and ready to serve.*

• *Include in your menu cold or room temperature salads or marinated vegetables that don't require oven time.*

• *Serve cold sliced ham as your entrée, and concentrate on making the other dishes warm and spectacular.*

• *Smoke or fry a turkey. (See recipes on pages 141 and 146.) This frees up your oven for side dishes and dessert.*

• *Enlist family members to bring dishes that have already been cooked. Reheat them briefly in the microwave before mealtime.*

• *Heat casseroles in the microwave, and finish in the oven just to crisp toppings.*

• *And keep in mind that a roasted turkey will stay hot under aluminum foil for up to 45 minutes. This allows you time to bake those last-minute side dishes.*

GREEN PEAS AND BABY LIMAS WITH PINE NUTS

Tender lima beans and petite peas cooked in chicken broth are even better with fresh rosemary and toasted pine nuts. And there's no need to thaw the peas or beans before cooking.

1 (14-ounce) can chicken broth
1 (10-ounce) package frozen baby lima beans
4½ cups frozen petite peas (1½ [16-ounce] packages)
½ teaspoon sugar
¾ cup pine nuts
2 tablespoons butter or margarine, melted
3 green onions, chopped
1 tablespoon chopped fresh rosemary
½ teaspoon salt
¼ teaspoon pepper
3 tablespoons butter or margarine

Bring broth to a boil in a saucepan; add lima beans. Return to a boil; cover, reduce heat, and simmer 15 minutes or until tender. Stir in peas and ½ teaspoon sugar; cook 2 minutes. Drain.

Sauté pine nuts in 2 tablespoons butter in a large skillet over medium heat until golden. Add bean mixture, green onions, and next 3 ingredients; cook 1 minute or until thoroughly heated. Stir in remaining 3 tablespoons butter until melted. Yield: 12 servings.

SWISS-SQUASH CASSEROLE

Yellow squash and Swiss cheese make a mild-mannered side dish that complements roast turkey and all the trimmings.

8 (½") French baguette slices
1 tablespoon butter or margarine, melted
4 pounds yellow squash, sliced (about 12 medium)
2 small onions, chopped
2 bay leaves
1 teaspoon salt
1 teaspoon ground black pepper
6 tablespoons butter or margarine
6 tablespoons all-purpose flour
3 cups milk
1 teaspoon seasoned salt
½ teaspoon dried thyme
¼ teaspoon ground red pepper
1 teaspoon white wine Worcestershire sauce
4 egg yolks, beaten
1½ cups (6 ounces) shredded Swiss cheese, divided

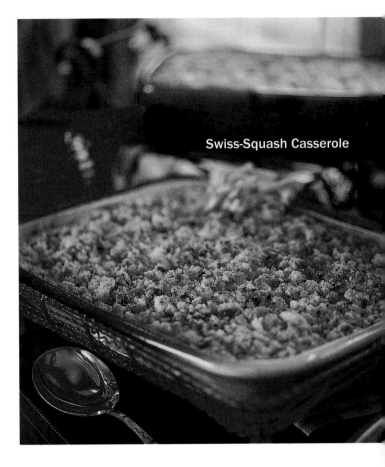

Swiss-Squash Casserole

Place baguette slices on an ungreased baking sheet; spread evenly with 1 tablespoon butter. Bake at 400° for 5 minutes or until crisp and golden. Let cool. Process in a blender or food processor until crumbs form. (This will yield about 1½ cups crumbs.) Set aside.

Place squash, onion, and bay leaves in a Dutch oven with a small amount of water. Bring to a boil; reduce heat, and simmer, uncovered, 10 minutes or until squash is tender. Drain, discarding bay leaves. Sprinkle squash with salt and pepper.

Melt 6 tablespoons butter in a 4-quart saucepan over medium heat. Whisk in flour until smooth. Cook 1 minute, whisking constantly. Gradually whisk in milk; cook over medium heat, stirring constantly, until thickened and bubbly. Remove from heat; stir in seasoned salt and next 3 ingredients. Gradually stir about one-fourth of hot white sauce into yolks; add to remaining hot white sauce, stirring constantly. Stir in 1 cup cheese.

Combine squash and cheese sauce. Spoon into a greased 2-quart baking dish. Combine remaining ½ cup cheese and reserved breadcrumbs; sprinkle over squash. Bake, uncovered, at 350° for 40 minutes or until browned. Yield: 12 servings.

Note: *If you can't find fresh yellow squash, substitute frozen sliced squash.*

GINGERSNAP SWEET POTATOES `Make Ahead`

A crisp gingersnap topping earns this Southern sweet potato casserole high marks. Purchase crisp gingersnap cookies rather than the soft variety for making the streusel.

6   sweet potatoes (4 pounds)
½   cup firmly packed light brown sugar
½   cup butter or margarine, melted
⅓   cup half-and-half
2   large eggs
1   teaspoon vanilla extract
½   cup firmly packed light brown sugar
2   tablespoons all-purpose flour
¼   cup cold butter or margarine, cut into pieces
32   coarsely crushed gingersnap cookies (we tested with Nabisco)

Cook sweet potatoes in a Dutch oven in boiling water to cover over medium heat 30 minutes or until tender. Cool; peel and mash potatoes.

Combine mashed sweet potato, ½ cup brown sugar, and next 4 ingredients in a mixing bowl; beat at medium speed with an electric mixer until smooth. (Or mash with a potato masher until smooth.) Spoon into a greased 2½-quart or 13" x 9" baking dish.

Combine ½ cup brown sugar and flour. Cut in ¼ cup cold butter with a pastry blender until crumbly. Stir in crushed gingersnaps. Sprinkle streusel over sweet potato. Bake, uncovered, at 350° for 25 minutes or until streusel is lightly browned. Yield: 10 servings.

Make Ahead: *Prepare sweet potato filling, and spoon into a greased 2½-quart microwave-safe dish. Cover and chill overnight. Microwave at HIGH 10 minutes or until hot. Prepare streusel, and sprinkle over filling. Bake, uncovered, at 350° for 20 minutes or until streusel is lightly browned.*

Gingersnap Sweet Potatoes

CRANBERRY-KUMQUAT RELISH `Make Ahead • Quick & Easy`

Kumquats add a citrus surprise to this favorite holiday sauce that you can make up to a week ahead.

1   (16-ounce) can whole-berry cranberry sauce
1   cup finely chopped kumquats (about 18)
6   tablespoons sugar
3   tablespoons coarse-grained mustard

Combine all ingredients in a saucepan over medium heat. Bring to a boil and cook, stirring often, 2 minutes or until sugar dissolves. Remove from heat. Cover and chill. Yield: about 3 cups.

CRANBERRY-LIME SHERBET `Make Ahead • Quick & Easy`

Three ingredients combine to make a refreshing light and tangy dessert for serving after a heavy meal.

3   cups cranberry-apple juice drink
1   (14-ounce) can sweetened condensed milk
1   cup fresh lime juice

Combine all ingredients; pour into an 8" square dish. Cover and freeze overnight or until firm. Cut frozen mixture into small squares. Process in a food processor, in 2 batches, until smooth. Place slush in a plastic container; cover and freeze at least 3 hours or until firm. Serve small scoops with sugar cookies or Christmas cookies, if desired. Yield: 6 cups.

See page 151 for Holiday Lane Cake recipe.

Holiday Lane Cake (page 151)
and Cranberry-Lime Sherbet

SPECIAL SETTINGS

The dining table is a common gathering spot at this time of year. The creative ideas shown on these pages will enhance the festive atmosphere and, no doubt, spark some interesting conversation as well.

▲ FIRE AND ICE CANDLES

Opposites definitely attract in this snowy candle creation. Place a candle and clear glass votive holder inside a large wine goblet. Fill in around the votive holder with white wax crystals (available at crafts stores).

◀ FRESH AND FESTIVE

White table linens accented with feathery evergreens set a serene mood. White candles and silver accessories make the setting sparkle. Long lengths of satiny ribbon criss-cross the table, adding a dressy detail. A silver metallic paint pen was used to write the word "Joy" on the ribbon.

A SWEET BOUQUET ▶

Flowers make a big impression when nestled behind the bow of this chair cover. To keep the flowers fresh for several hours, wrap wet paper towels around the cut stems; then completely cover the paper towels with florist tape. The flowers can be easily lifted out and given as a party favor.

▲ 5-MINUTE TABLE RUNNER

Add a handsome trim to your table in no time. Position a length of fabric down the center of your table and turn under the raw edges. Gather the fabric ends in a ribbon bow. Wire together a nosegay of berries and greenery, and tuck it behind the knot of the bow.

FROSTY BERRY CENTERPIECE ▶

A tall glass vase filled with cranberries and faux snow sets a Christmassy tone. For the vase topper shown here, tuck flowers and greenery into a florist foam block. Place pillar candles in the center of the arrangement. For a simpler centerpiece, skip the flowers and place a large pillar candle securely among the cranberries.

PRETTY PAPERS

Perfect for a child's party (or the young at heart!), these table decorations rely on paper products for their whimsical charm. Lengths of wrapping paper do double duty as table runners and place mats. The ends are trimmed with raffia tied through holes punched in the paper. Buckets filled with party favors are tied onto each chair.

A frilly ruff of red shredded paper is sandwiched between a gold charger and the white dinner plate. A cone that can later serve as an ornament makes a tidy napkin holder.

TIPS FOR TABLE SETTINGS

Imaginative table settings are a fun way to express the mood of your dinner party. Before you add your own creative flair, however, here are some basic tips to follow for getting everything in its proper place.

• If place mats are used, place them flush with the table edge or about one inch from the edge.

• Place the dinner plate and flatware about one inch from the edge of the table.

• As a rule for flatware, start from the outside and work your way in. That is, the flatware for the first course is on the outside, farthest from the plate.

• Keep the amount of flatware that will be used to a minimum. Generally, there should be no more than three pieces of flatware on each side of the plate.

• Put the knife and spoons to the right of the plate, with the knife's cutting edge facing the plate. Forks go to the left of the plate.

• The dessert fork or spoon can be brought in with the dessert or placed European style (above the dinner plate).

• Fold the napkin, and lay it on the place mat to the left of the forks.

• Place the water glass above the knife. Position additional glasses next to the water glass in order of use.

• Place bread-and-butter plates near the tip of the dinner fork. If there is no bread-and-butter plate, place the salad plate there instead.

• If there is a bread-and-butter plate, place the salad plate to the left and a little below the bread-and-butter plate.

individual butter spreader

dessert spoon or dessert fork

water glass

tea or wine glass

bread-and-butter plate

service plate or charger

napkin

soup spoon

dinner plate

salad plate

dinner fork

dinner knife

cup and saucer

salad fork

teaspoon

◀ CITRUS DELIGHTS

Stacked pedestal dishes are an easy solution for a center-piece. Here, citrus fruits accented with ribbons, bits of Fraser fir, and hypericum berries create a happy display.

To make the candleholders, slice off the top end of the fruit, and cut around the inside perimeter with a sharp knife. Scoop out enough pulp so that a small votive candle or tea light fits inside the fruit. Tuck moss around the candle. Nestle the fruit in a juice glass filled with jelly beans. Be careful to keep the candle flame away from the moss, and never leave burning candles unattended.

▲ EASY BEGINNINGS

An evergreen wreath is a good start to a great centerpiece. Stand a holiday motif statue in the center of the wreath, and you have an instant table decoration.

PRETTY IN RED AND GREEN

A tall ivy tree decorated with ornaments and twirling ribbons dominates
this lushly decorated dining room. Abundant evergreen garlands are a
Christmassy complement to the red tablecloth and red and white flowers.

◀ STYLISH DETAILS

Crisscross wide ribbon on chair seats to create the illusion of a wrapped package. The chair pictured has a seat that can be unscrewed and lifted off easily, so the ribbon fits neatly around the seat cushion; or you can just wrap the ribbon around the entire seat. A ribbon tied to the chair back completes the look.

TABLETOP GREETINGS ▼

Glue thin cording and leaf embellishments to vintage postcards to make unique place cards. Leave extra cording at the top for a hanger, and the card can be hung on the tree as a memento of a lovely dinner.

GIFTS & WRAPPINGS

Show how much you care with handsome gifts and wrappings that you make yourself.

15 UNFORGETTABLE WRAPS

*There's something so delightful and intriguing about packages piled
under the tree. It doesn't take lots of expensive materials to
put together great wraps—just some trimmings and a little creativity.*

BURLAP BUNDLES
These clever little wrappings make the perfect cover-up for presents
that won't quite fit in a box. Begin by cutting a square of burlap and
fringing the edges. Gather the sides of the burlap, secure with a rubber band, and tie with a velvet ribbon.

PACKAGES BY POST

Printed postcards, popular in the early 1900s, usually reflected
Victorian holiday themes and were either mailed or used as calling
cards. These classic cards add a vintage touch when tied or glued to
packages and gift bags.

FIT TO BE TIED

Give gift bags a new look by tying the entire bag with ribbon instead of just the handle. Cut a small slit at the top of one side of the bag. Tape one end of a wide length of ribbon to the bottom of the bag, slide the ribbon through the slit, and let it hang over the other side. Embellish the ensemble with more ribbon, candy, and greenery.

▲ CLIP-ON TAGS

Colorful Christmas fabrics and painted clothespins are the simple secret behind these personality-packed packages. Take the clothespins apart to paint them. Once they're dry, use a paint pen to write a message on the pins. Then wrap the gift with fabric and clip the bundle together using the clothespins.

CHRISTMAS CANDY CAN ▶

Look no further than your cupboard to create this crafty container. Glue wide red ribbon and thin green ribbon onto a coffee can. Trim the top and bottom with rickrack. Twist together two lengths of soldering wire to make a handle. Punch holes in the can at opposite sides and attach the wire handle. To remove the label from your can, soak it in warm soapy water for an hour.

TAGS IN A TWINKLING

These felt tags are made with the patterns on page 172. Transfer each pattern onto a doubled piece of felt and cut out. Blanket stitch the two felt pieces together using embroidery floss. For the heart and tree tags, cut a heart and a star from vellum. Write the recipient's name on the vellum and stitch it onto the felt. For the stocking, cut two pieces of felt for the stocking cuff and stitch the receiver's name on one piece. Stitch the front and back cuff pieces onto the stocking.

▲ PACKED WITH PUNCH

Brightly colored craft foam is ideal for creating whimsical package accents. Use the foam to make custom handles for gift sacks. Fasten the handles to the bags with metal paper fasteners. Decorate the handles with craft-foam snowflakes or dots made by punching holes in the foam. Top each bag with a craft-foam tag.

◀ TRIMMED WITH TREES

Make fun tags by cutting two pieces of craft foam into tree shapes and sandwiching cellophane paper shreds between them. Place a ribbon streamer from the package bow between the front and back tree pieces and glue together.

▲ CHRISTMAS CASES

Personalize CDs by designing your own case covers. The options for decorations are limitless. Use hand-made papers, decorative papers, stickers, ribbons, and even your computer to make a custom cover.

◀ THE ENVELOPE PLEASE

Present gift certificates, money, or tickets in a felt pouch. To create it, cut a rectangle of felt wide enough for your gift and long enough to fold up from the bottom for the pocket and over at the top for the flap. Glue the sides together. Trim the flap with a scalloped design. Cut a piece of felt in a contrasting color slightly larger than the flap, and glue it to the back side of the flap. Sew a button to the envelope pocket, and cut a buttonhole in the flap.

◀ A LITTLE SOMETHING EXTRA

Craft a special detail for your gift ties by threading decorative beads onto cording or ribbon streamers. Knot the ribbon at the bottom of the beads to hold them in place. Beads can be found at crafts and discount stores. Pieces of old costume jewelry are also a great source for beautiful package trims.

▼ TAKE OUT A TREASURE

Pack clear carryout containers, traditionally used by Asian restaurants, with paper shreds. (Make your own paper filler by shredding newspapers, magazines, or grocery bags.) Hide a little gift inside and top the container with colorful ribbon.

RICKRACK WRAP

A quick stop by the fabric store can provide you with great trimmings for holiday packages. Wrap lengths of jumbo rickrack around a bright package and hot-glue the ends to the back. Cover a button form with coordinating fabric, and hot-glue the button to the center of a ribbon bow. Glue the bow onto the package.

▲ TASSEL TRIM

Here's a great use for pretty ribbon scraps. Cover a small craft foam ball with fabric, trimming the fabric as needed to fit smoothly around the ball. Glue the fabric in place. Glue narrow ribbon to the ball to cover any fabric seams. Run a narrow ribbon up through the foam ball and back down again. Knot at the bottom, leaving a 2-inch loop at the top. Cut 10-inch pieces of assorted ribbon. Pull the knot down from the foam ball and thread ribbon through the opening. Once all the ribbon has been threaded, pull the loop at the top of the tassel.

◄ MONOGRAMMED RIBBONS

Add personalized elegance to a gift tied with velvet ribbon by embellishing it with a monogram. Simply glue iron-on monogram letters onto the ribbon.

GIFTS FROM THE HEART

This year add a little handmade charm to your gifts.
Here are a few ideas for some one-of-a-kind treasures
that will convey heartfelt sentiments of the season.

BEADED CARDS

Transform beads and handmade paper into dazzling Christmas cards. Draw the desired shape onto double adhesive paper and cut it out. Stick the shape to the front of the card. Peel off the remaining side of the adhesive and pour on the beads. If you are using ribbon, press the ribbon on before you place the beads. Press the beads to make sure they are secure.

FANCY NAPKIN RINGS

Craft a set of napkin rings to give as a hostess gift. Cut the cardboard tube from a paper towel roll down the long side. Cut fabric into 6 (5- x 8½-inch) pieces and brush fabric stiffener on both sides. Fold the long sides of each fabric piece to the back so that the ends meet in the middle. Position each fabric piece, seam side down, onto a section of paper towel roll that has been trimmed to the size of the fabric. Let dry overnight. Hot-glue beads and trims to the inside of each ring. Hot-glue each ring together, overlapping ends. To present, thread the napkin rings on a ribbon and include a gift tag.

▲ HOLIDAY HERBS

Present a pot of herbs to the cook or gardener on your list. Personalize a plain terra-cotta pot by covering the rim with tape and painting the bottom of the pot with a water-diluted acrylic paint mixture. Once dry, remove the tape from the rim and place tape just underneath the rim. Paint the rim with chalkboard paint. Use chalk to write a message.

◀ PICTURE THIS TRAY

One of the greatest things about handcrafting gifts is turning an ordinary item into something special. With just a few simple additions, a picture frame transforms into a tray. Simply cut a piece of fabric to cover the cardboard insert inside the frame. Attach drawer pulls to the sides of the frame to use as handles for a picture-perfect gift.

DAINTY TIE-ONS ▶

Design a set of gift tags by embellishing thick paper with remnants of ribbons and trims and even tiny pinecones and greenery sprigs.

CHRISTMAS COMFORT FOOD GIFTS

Decadent dessert sauces, munchy candy mix,
a warm loaf of bread, and homemade pimiento cheese—
these are feel-good foods worthy of gift giving all year long.

Granola Gorp

GRANOLA GORP `Make Ahead`

A bunch of healthy ingredients (and a little bit of candy) create this addicting, go-anywhere snack. Omit the peanuts and candies, and enjoy it for breakfast.

4	cups uncooked regular oats
½	cup honey wheat germ
½	cup sunflower kernels
⅓	cup sesame seeds
¼	cup firmly packed light brown sugar
⅓	cup honey
⅓	cup vegetable oil
¼	cup creamy peanut butter
1	teaspoon vanilla extract
1	(9.4-ounce) package candy-coated milk chocolate pieces
1	cup raisins
1	cup unsalted roasted peanuts

Combine first 5 ingredients in a large bowl. Combine honey and next 3 ingredients; pour over dry ingredients, and toss to coat. Spread in 2 greased 15" x 10" jellyroll pans. Bake at 325° for 20 minutes, stirring after 10 minutes and again after 15 minutes. Cool. Stir in candy, raisins, and peanuts. Package gorp for gift giving. Yield: 9¾ cups.

DRIED FRUIT CHUTNEY

Fresh rosemary brings out the best in this sweet and savory fruit chutney. Make our Wintery White Wine Punch first (page 156), saving the strained fruit for this recipe.

2	tablespoons butter or margarine
1	celery rib, finely chopped
1	onion, finely chopped
1	garlic clove, minced
	Reserved strained fruit from Wintery White Wine Punch (page 156)
½	cup chopped pecans, toasted
1	tablespoon brown sugar
1	cup thawed apple juice concentrate (about ½ [12-ounce] container)
1	(5") sprig fresh rosemary

Melt butter in a Dutch oven over medium heat. Add celery, onion, and garlic; cook 8 to 10 minutes or until very tender.

Remove and discard orange slices from fruit mixture; coarsely chop fruit.

Add chopped fruit and remaining ingredients to vegetables. Bring to a boil; cover, reduce heat to low, and cook 1 hour and 40 minutes or until fruit is very tender and most of liquid has been absorbed, stirring occasionally. Remove rosemary sprig and discard. Serve chutney with roasted poultry, pork, or other meats. Yield: 4 cups.

SILKY FUDGE SAUCE

Smooth as silk, yet thick and fudgy—a taste of this sauce is like eating candy.

½	cup butter or margarine
1	(4-ounce) sweet chocolate bar, chopped (we tested with Baker's German Sweet)
1	cup sugar
1	(5-ounce) can evaporated milk
1	tablespoon light corn syrup
⅛	teaspoon salt
1	teaspoon vanilla extract

Melt butter and chocolate in a heavy saucepan over medium-low heat. Stir in sugar, evaporated milk, corn syrup, and salt; cook over medium heat, stirring gently, 5 minutes or just until sugar dissolves and sauce is smooth. Remove from heat; stir in vanilla. Cool to room temperature. Pour into gift jars. Cover and chill up to 1 month. Serve warm. Yield: 2 cups.

Note: *Reheat 1 cup sauce in a glass jar without lid in microwave at MEDIUM (50% power) 2 minutes, stirring after 1 minute. (For testing, we used an 1100-watt microwave oven.)*

SAUCY SERVING SUGGESTIONS

- Serve fudge sauce warm over ice cream, toasted pound cake slices, waffles, or plain storebought cheesecake.

- Serve sauce slightly warm as fondue with strawberries, pineapple chunks, marshmallows, and graham crackers for dippers.

- Blend a few tablespoons of fudge sauce into softened vanilla ice cream for a rich milk shake.

- Stir a few tablespoons of fudge sauce into a cold glass of milk or a hot cup of coffee.

**Caramel-White Chocolate Sauce
and Silky Fudge Sauce**

CARAMEL-WHITE CHOCOLATE SAUCE

You won't see the white chocolate in this thick sauce, but you'll know it's there when you take a taste and experience the sublime buttery flavor.

1   cup water
2   cups sugar
1   cup heavy whipping cream
1   teaspoon vanilla extract
⅛   teaspoon salt
1   (4-ounce) premium white chocolate baking bar, chopped (we tested with Ghirardelli)

Pour water into a large heavy saucepan. Add sugar to center of saucepan. Cover and bring to a boil over high heat. Uncover; attach a candy thermometer to side of pan, and cook about 15 minutes or until thermometer registers 300°. Reduce heat to medium; cook about 5 more minutes or until thermometer registers 350°.

Meanwhile, bring whipping cream to a simmer in a small saucepan. Remove caramel syrup from heat. Carefully add about half of hot cream to caramel (mixture will bubble up). Gradually add remaining cream, vanilla, and salt; let bubbling subside. Add white chocolate (it will look like it's going to separate); whisk gently until smooth. Cool to room temperature. Pour into gift jars. Cover and chill up to 1 month. Serve warm. Yield: 2⅓ cups.

Note: Reheat 1 cup sauce in a glass jar without lid in microwave at MEDIUM (50% power) 2 minutes, stirring after 1 minute. (For testing, we used an 1100-watt microwave oven.)

STREUSEL-TOPPED BANANA NUT BREAD

Bake these little loaves in disposable pans from the grocery store or in baking molds. We tell you how in the Note at right.

½   cup firmly packed light brown sugar
7   tablespoons uncooked regular oats
⅓   cup all-purpose flour
⅓   cup cold butter or margarine, cut into pieces
2   small ripe bananas, mashed (1 cup)
2   large eggs
½   cup sugar
⅓   cup butter or margarine, melted
1½ cups all-purpose flour
1½ teaspoons baking powder
¾   teaspoon baking soda
¼   teaspoon salt
1   cup chopped pecans, toasted
1   teaspoon vanilla extract

Combine first 3 ingredients. Cut in ⅓ cup butter with a pastry blender until crumbly; chill streusel.

Beat banana and next 3 ingredients in a large mixing bowl at medium speed with an electric mixer 1 minute or just until smooth.

Combine 1½ cups flour and next 3 ingredients. Add to banana, beating just until dry ingredients are moistened. Stir in pecans and vanilla.

Spoon batter into 3 (5¾" x 3¼") greased disposable mini loafpans. Sprinkle each loaf evenly with streusel. Bake at 350° for 35 minutes. Cool in pans on a wire rack 5 minutes; carefully remove from pans, and cool on wire rack. Return loaves to pans for gift giving. Yield: 3 mini loaves.

Note: *We also loved using these 7" x 4" wooden baking molds for gift giving. You'll get 2 loaves using the recipe above. For baking, line molds with paper inserts, fill with batter, place molds on a baking sheet and bake 45 minutes. When cool, wrap each loaf in plastic wrap. Wrap a strip of parchment paper around plastic wrap, using the parchment as a gift tag. Tie with ribbon.*

Streusel-Topped Banana Nut Bread

No-Bake Jumbo Peanut Butter Cookies

NO-BAKE PEANUT BUTTER COOKIES

Make Ahead • Quick & Easy

Need a quick gift? Stir these chocolate, peanut butter, and oat cookies together in no time.

2   cups sugar
¼   cup cocoa
½   cup butter or margarine
½   cup milk
½   teaspoon vanilla extract
½   cup creamy or crunchy peanut butter
3   cups uncooked quick-cooking oats

Combine first 5 ingredients in a medium saucepan. Cook over low heat until butter melts, stirring occasionally. Increase heat to medium; bring to a boil. Boil 1 minute. Remove from heat; quickly stir in peanut butter until smooth. Stir in oats. Quickly drop by heaping tablespoonfuls onto wax paper. Let cool completely. Carefully remove from wax paper. Store in an airtight container. Yield: 4 dozen.

Jumbo Cookies: *Quickly drop cookie dough by ¼ cupfuls onto wax paper.*

HOMEMADE PIMIENTO CHEESE

This spicy cheese gets its kick from pickled jalapeños. For best results with this classic spread, shred your own cheese instead of using preshredded cheese. Let the spread sit at room temperature to soften before slathering it on a sandwich.

1½ cups mayonnaise (we tested with Duke's)
1   (4-ounce) jar diced pimiento, drained
1   tablespoon finely grated onion
1   teaspoon Worcestershire sauce
1   (8-ounce) block extra-sharp Cheddar cheese, shredded
1   (8-ounce) block sharp Cheddar cheese, shredded
½   cup pickled jalapeño pepper slices, drained and chopped

Combine first 4 ingredients in a large bowl; stir in cheeses. Stir in chopped pepper. Spoon cheese into gift jars. Store in refrigerator. Yield: about 4 cups.

Note: *To blend in the shredded cheeses more easily, first let them sit at room temperature for 20 to 30 minutes to soften.*

Homemade Pimiento Cheese

TEST KITCHENS' TOP 10
GADGET GIFTS

The coolest tools to hit the kitchen are revealed here,
each one put to work producing a delicious holiday treat.
We show you how to package them all as gifts.

CHOCOLATE MALT CAKE

Malted milk balls and chocolate syrup make this moist snack cake scrumptious. A food chopper makes quick work of chopping the malted milk ball topping.

½	cup butter or margarine, softened
1	cup sugar
4	large eggs
1	teaspoon vanilla extract
1	cup all-purpose flour
2	tablespoons malted milk powder (we tested with Carnation)
½	teaspoon salt
½	cup chocolate syrup (we tested with Hershey's)
½	cup butter or margarine, softened
2	cups sifted powdered sugar
1	teaspoon malted milk powder
1	cup (6 ounces) semisweet chocolate morsels
¼	cup butter or margarine
1½	cups chopped malted milk balls (see Note)

Beat ½ cup butter at medium speed with an electric mixer until creamy; add 1 cup sugar, beating well. Add eggs and vanilla; beat well. Combine flour, 2 tablespoons malted milk powder, and salt; add to butter mixture, beating well. Stir in chocolate syrup.

Pour batter into a greased 13" x 9" pan. Bake at 350° for 28 minutes or until a wooden pick inserted in center comes out clean. Cool completely in pan on a wire rack.

Beat ½ cup butter at medium speed until creamy; add powdered sugar and 1 teaspoon malted milk powder, beating until smooth. (Add a little milk for spreadable consistency, if necessary.) Spread frosting over cooled cake.

Combine chocolate morsels and ¼ cup butter in a small saucepan; cook over low heat until chocolate and butter melt, stirring often. Cool 5 minutes; spread over frosted cake. Sprinkle with chopped malted milk balls, pressing gently into frosting and glaze. Cover and chill cake 1 hour before serving. Yield: 12 servings.

Note: *To get the best results chopping malted milk balls, freeze the candy; then chop in small batches in a food chopper.*

CHERRY AND WHITE CHOCOLATE OATMEAL COOKIES

Studded with sweetened dried cherries and chunks of white chocolate, these chewy cookies make a really good first impression. A cookie scoop makes it easy to portion out little mounds of dough.

1   cup butter or margarine, softened
1   cup firmly packed light brown sugar
¾   cup sugar
2   large eggs
1   tablespoon vanilla extract
2   cups all-purpose flour
2   teaspoons baking powder
½   teaspoon baking soda
½   teaspoon salt
2   cups uncooked regular oats
2   (6-ounce) packages white chocolate baking bars, coarsely chopped (we tested with Baker's)
1   cup sweetened dried cherries (we tested with Mariani)

Beat butter at medium speed with an electric mixer until fluffy; gradually add sugars, beating well. Add eggs and vanilla; beat well.

Combine flour and next 3 ingredients; gradually add to butter mixture, beating well. Stir in oats, white chocolate, and cherries.

Using 1 tablespoon cookie scoop, drop dough 2" apart onto ungreased baking sheets. Bake at 375° for 10 minutes or until lightly browned. Cool 2 minutes on pans; remove to wire racks to cool. Yield: 5 dozen.

COOKIE SCOOP

Use this all-purpose scoop for portioning out dough and for making ice cream balls, and sorbet and melon balls, too. **For gift giving,** *wrap a stack of cookies tightly in plastic wrap; then wrap stack in parchment paper and secure with tape. Tie with ribbon, attaching scoop through ribbon. Add greenery.*

Cherry and White Chocolate Oatmeal Cookies

SWISS CHARD TARTLETS

Sesame seeds are a pleasant surprise in this pastry while Gouda cheese and Swiss chard make a tasty filling. See the Note on freezing these savory pastries. Give freshly baked or frozen pastries and the pans as a gift, and include directions for reheating in a gift card.

1½   cups all-purpose flour
3   tablespoons sesame seeds
1   teaspoon salt, divided
½   cup cold butter, cut into pieces
4½   tablespoons ice water
1   tablespoon olive oil
1   garlic clove, sliced
5   cups coarsely chopped Swiss chard leaves (about 1
      large bunch)
1   cup half-and-half
2   large eggs
¼   teaspoon pepper
½   cup (2 ounces) shredded Gouda cheese

Pulse flour, sesame seeds, and ¾ teaspoon salt in a food processor 3 or 4 times or just until combined. Add butter through food chute, and pulse 5 or 6 times or until crumbly. Gradually add 4½ tablespoons water, pulsing 3 or 4 times or just until dough forms a soft ball.

Divide dough into 6 portions and flatten each portion into a disk. Cover and chill dough 30 minutes. Roll each disk to ⅛" thickness; fit into 6 individual 4" quiche pans or tart pans with removable bottoms; trim off excess pastry along edges. Place in freezer 30 minutes. Bake at 400° for 10 to 12 minutes or until golden. Set aside.

Meanwhile, heat oil in a large skillet over medium heat until hot. Add garlic, and cook 30 seconds or until golden. Discard garlic. Increase heat to medium-high; add chopped chard, and sauté 5 minutes or until tender and moisture is absorbed. Set aside.

Whisk together half-and-half and eggs. Stir in remaining ¼ teaspoon salt and pepper.

Place tartlets on a baking sheet; divide chard evenly among shells. Fill with egg mixture to within ½" of tops. Sprinkle each tartlet with 1 heaping tablespoon cheese. Bake at 400° for 20 minutes or until set and lightly browned. Yield: 6 tartlets.

Note: *Baked tartlets can be sealed in zip-top freezer bags and frozen. Reheat straight from the freezer at 350° for 25 minutes or until thoroughly heated.*

Swiss Chard Tartlets

4" QUICHE PANS

Give a gift stack of these little pans with removable bottoms. They're great for baking sweet or savory tarts. **For gift giving,** *stack tartlets with cardboard rounds between each one. Wrap stack in cellophane or plastic wrap. Tie with cheesecloth. Add holly.*

BAKING MAT

The beauty of a nonstick baking mat is that it never needs greasing, it releases food easily, and it has simple wipe-clean appeal. Just wipe with a damp sponge. **For gift giving,** stack wafers between wax paper, wrap stacks of wafers in cellophane and tie with ribbon. Fold baking mat and tie with ribbon. Add rosemary sprig. Tuck wafers in each end.

Herbed
Parmesan Wafers

HERBED PARMESAN WAFERS

Fresh rosemary, pine nuts, and almonds flatter these lacy cheese wafers. Lifting a delicate baked wafer isn't a problem when you line your baking sheet with a nonstick mat. And you skip greasing the pan.

1   cup coarsely grated Parmigiano-Reggiano cheese
    (see Note)
1/3 cup sliced almonds
2   tablespoons chopped pine nuts
2   teaspoons chopped fresh rosemary

Line a baking sheet with a nonstick baking mat. Combine all ingredients in a bowl.

Divide cheese mixture evenly into 4 piles on a work surface. Working with one portion at a time, divide pile evenly into 5 smaller piles, placing them at least 1" apart on baking mat. Gently flatten each pile into a 2" to 2½" circle, making sure there are no large holes.

Bake at 400° for 4 to 5 minutes or just until edges are browned and wafers are bubbly throughout; remove from oven. Working quickly, carefully transfer hot wafers with a thin spatula to a cooling rack. Cool completely. Repeat process with remaining cheese mixture. Yield: 20 wafers.

Jumbo Cheese Wafer: *You can also make 1 large cheese wafer. Break it into pieces after it cools, and sprinkle on top of salads or into tomato or French onion soup. To make 1 large wafer, prepare cheese mixture and place entire amount on baking mat to form a 10½" x 8½" rectangle. Bake at 400° for 7 to 8 minutes or just until edges are brown and wafer is bubbly throughout.*

Note: *Get coarsely grated cheese by using the largest holes of a box grater.*

WALNUT TART

Spiced rum and walnuts make this tart a statement of sweet simplicity. A tart pan with a removable bottom is a good baking investment.

1   cup all-purpose flour
2   tablespoons sugar
¼   teaspoon salt
¼   cup cold butter or margarine, cut into pieces
3   to 4 tablespoons ice water
1   cup firmly packed light brown sugar
½   cup butter or margarine, softened
1   large egg
2   tablespoons spiced rum
2   cups chopped walnuts

Pulse first 3 ingredients in a food processor 3 or 4 times or until combined. Add ¼ cup butter, and pulse 5 or 6 times or until crumbly. With processor running, gradually add water, and process until dough comes together and leaves sides of bowl. Shape dough into a 1"-thick disk. Cover and chill 15 minutes.

Roll pastry to ⅛" thickness on a lightly floured surface. Fit into an ungreased 9" tart pan; trim off excess pastry along edges. Place pan in freezer 15 minutes.

Line pastry with parchment paper, and fill with pie weights or dried beans. Bake at 450° for 5 minutes. Remove parchment paper and pie weights. Bake 6 more minutes or until crust is lightly browned. Set aside. Reduce oven temperature to 325°.

Beat 1 cup brown sugar and ½ cup butter at medium speed with an electric mixer 1 minute or until creamy. Add egg and rum, beating just until combined. Stir in walnuts. Spread filling into pastry shell.

Bake at 325° for 45 minutes or until browned. Cool in pan on a wire rack. Yield: 1 (9") tart.

Walnut Tart

9" TART PAN

Tart pans are a great gift for baking sweet and savory dishes. Want to give a little something extra to go along with the pan? Add a jar of pie weights. **For gift giving,** *wrap tart in plastic wrap, place wrapped tart on a metal tray; anchor with ribbon. Tie ribbon around jar of pie weights, and add to tray.*

Orange Scones with Dates

ORANGE SCONES WITH DATES

A Microplane® grater produces feathery fine orange zest to flavor these tender scones. They're at their best when warm from the oven.

2   cups all-purpose flour
¼   cup sugar
1   tablespoon baking powder
1   teaspoon ground cardamom (see Note)
¼   teaspoon salt
⅓   cup cold butter, cut into pieces
¾   cup chopped dates
½   cup heavy whipping cream
1   large egg, beaten
2   tablespoons orange zest
1   tablespoon heavy whipping cream
Sugar

Combine first 5 ingredients in a bowl; cut in butter with a pastry blender until crumbly. Stir in dates. Stir together ½ cup whipping cream, egg, and orange zest; add to dry ingredients, stirring with a fork until dry ingredients are moistened.

Gather dough into a ball. Pat dough into an 8" circle on an ungreased baking sheet. Cut dough into 8 wedges using a sharp knife, cutting to, but not through, bottom of dough. Brush tops with 1 tablespoon whipping cream; sprinkle with sugar.

Bake at 350° for 23 minutes. Serve warm. Yield: 8 scones.

Note: *Cardamom is not as commonly used as other baking spices. It has a warm, spicy-sweet flavor, and a little goes a long way. It pairs nicely with orange and dates in these scones, but the scones taste great if you choose to omit it.*

CAESAR SALAD DRESSING

Caesar dressing is a salad classic. For food safety, our version replaces the traditional raw egg with egg substitute.

½   cup egg substitute
½   cup red wine vinegar
¼   cup fresh lemon juice
2   teaspoons Worcestershire sauce
1   (2-ounce) can anchovies, drained
5   garlic cloves, coarsely chopped
1   tablespoon Dijon mustard
½   teaspoon freshly ground black pepper
¼   teaspoon ground red pepper
1   cup olive oil
¼   cup freshly grated Parmesan cheese

Process first 9 ingredients in a food processor until smooth, stopping twice to scrape down sides. With processor running, gradually add oil through food chute, processing just until combined. Stir in cheese. Cover and store in refrigerator up to 1 week. Yield: 2⅔ cups.

Caesar Salad Dressing

Streusel-Topped Pumpkin
Muffins

MUFFIN TOP PAN

Here's a novel gift for those who enjoy eating the top only of crunchy muffins and frosted cupcakes. **For gift giving,** *wrap pan of muffins in cellophane. Tie with ribbon, attaching long cinnamon sticks and greenery.*

STREUSEL-TOPPED PUMPKIN MUFFINS

Muffin tops are indeed the best part of the bread, especially when it means a streusel packed with pecans and brown sugar. Muffin top pans allow you to indulge with this holiday quick bread.

⅓   cup shortening

1   cup sugar

2   large eggs

1⅔ cups all-purpose flour

1   teaspoon baking powder

¼   teaspoon baking soda

½   teaspoon salt

½   teaspoon ground cinnamon

¼   teaspoon ground cloves

1   cup canned, mashed pumpkin

⅓   cup water

½   cup chopped pecans

1   teaspoon vanilla extract

½   cup uncooked regular oats

½   cup all-purpose flour

½   cup firmly packed light brown sugar

¼   cup cold butter or margarine, cut into pieces

½   cup chopped pecans

Beat shortening at medium speed with an electric mixer until creamy; gradually add 1 cup sugar, beating well. Add eggs, 1 at a time, beating until blended after each addition.

Combine 1⅔ cups flour and next 5 ingredients; add to shortening mixture alternately with pumpkin and water, beginning and ending with flour mixture. Beat at low speed until blended after each addition. Stir in ½ cup pecans and vanilla. Spoon into greased muffin top pans, filling three-fourths full.

Combine oats, ½ cup flour, and brown sugar. Cut in butter with a pastry blender until crumbly; stir in ½ cup pecans. Sprinkle streusel over batter. Bake at 375° for 22 minutes or until a wooden pick inserted in center comes out clean. Cool in pans on a wire rack 5 minutes. Remove from pans, and cool on wire racks. Yield: 1 dozen.

Note: *If you don't have a muffin top pan, spoon batter into regular 2½" muffin pans, filling two-thirds full. Bake at 375° for 20 minutes or until a wooden pick inserted in center comes out clean. Yield: 1½ dozen.*

Little Milk Chocolate
Cheesecakes

MINI SPRINGFORM PANS

Give a pair of these nifty nonstick pans as a gift with the cheesecakes baked right in them, along with a copy of the recipe for two. **For gift packaging,** *wrap 2 cheesecakes in cellophane; tie with ribbon, braid, and faux berries. Include recipe card and a bag of coffee beans.*

LITTLE MILK CHOCOLATE CHEESECAKES

A coffee-graham cracker crust enhances these rich chocolate cheesecakes that need no adornment. Package a pair as a gift in these cute pans along with a bag of coffee beans.

6   tablespoons butter or margarine
1⅔ cups graham cracker crumbs
⅓   cup sugar
1   tablespoon instant coffee or espresso granules (we tested with Café Bustelo)
2   (8-ounce) packages cream cheese, softened
1   (3-ounce) package cream cheese, softened
1   (8-ounce) container sour cream
½   cup sugar
3   large eggs
1   (11.5-ounce) package milk chocolate morsels, melted and cooled (we tested with Hershey's)
1   teaspoon vanilla extract

Melt butter in saucepan over medium heat. Remove from heat; stir in graham cracker crumbs, ⅓ cup sugar, and coffee granules. Press evenly into bottoms of 6 ungreased 4" mini springform pans. Place pans on a baking sheet. Bake at 350° for 6 to 8 minutes; cool. Reduce oven temperature to 325°.

Combine cream cheeses, sour cream, and ½ cup sugar. Beat at medium speed with an electric mixer until blended. Add eggs, 1 at a time, beating just until blended after each addition. Stir in melted chocolate and vanilla. Pour filling into pans. Bake at 325° for 21 to 23 minutes or just until set. (Cheesecakes will firm as they chill.) Cool to room temperature. Chill until ready to wrap and give as gifts. Yield: 6 (4") cheesecakes.

LITTLE MILK CHOCOLATE CHEESECAKES FOR TWO

2   tablespoons butter or margarine
½   cup graham cracker crumbs
2   tablespoons sugar
1   teaspoon instant coffee or espresso granules (we tested with Café Bustelo)
2   (3-ounce) packages cream cheese, softened
⅓   cup sour cream
3   tablespoons sugar
1   large egg
½   cup milk chocolate morsels, melted and cooled (we tested with Hershey's)
½   teaspoon vanilla extract

Melt butter in saucepan over medium heat. Remove from heat; stir in graham cracker crumbs, 2 tablespoons sugar, and coffee granules. Press evenly into bottoms of 2 ungreased 4" mini springform pans. Place pans on a baking sheet. Bake at 350° for 6 to 8 minutes; cool. Reduce oven temperature to 325°.

Combine cream cheese, sour cream, and 3 tablespoons sugar. Beat at medium speed with an electric mixer until blended. Add egg, beating just until blended. Stir in melted chocolate and vanilla. Pour filling into pans. Bake at 325° for 21 to 23 minutes or just until set. Cool to room temperature. Chill until ready to serve. Yield: 2 cheesecakes.

VANILLA BEAN PANCAKES

Shapely pancake molds and vanilla bean batter make this recipe and gift idea novel.

2   cups all-purpose flour
¼   cup sugar
1   tablespoon baking powder
½   teaspoon salt
1   vanilla bean
2   cups milk
2   tablespoons vegetable oil
1   large egg, lightly beaten

For gift giving, combine first 4 ingredients in a jar or zip-top plastic bag. Seal jar or bag. Attach vanilla bean to gift. Include recipe directions in a gift card.

To prepare pancakes, place dry ingredients in a large bowl, and make a well in center.

Split vanilla bean, and scrape seeds into a small bowl. Whisk in milk, oil, and egg until blended. Add to dry ingredients, stirring just until blended.

Place pancake molds on a hot, lightly greased griddle. Spray molds with cooking spray. Pour ¼ cup batter into each mold, spreading batter evenly to edges. Cook until tops are covered with bubbles and pancakes pull away from sides of molds; remove pancake molds. Turn pancakes and cook other side. Repeat process with remaining batter. Yield: 12 (4") pancakes.

Note: *To make these pancakes without pancake molds, drop batter by ¼ cupfuls onto a lightly greased hot griddle, and cook as directed above.*

Shortcut Solution: *For a quick gift idea, give a box of biscuit and pancake mix, flavored syrup, and the pancake molds.*

Vanilla Bean Pancakes

PANCAKE MOLDS

These molds make eating pancakes fun. Their nonstick coating makes them easy to use and easy to clean. **For gift giving,** *pour dry mix in a jar. Add lid and parchment paper cutout, if desired. Tie ribbon onto each mold. Tie molds together on top of jar, letting molds dangle off sides. Wrap wide ribbon around jar lid to hold molds in place. Tuck vanilla bean into wide ribbon.*

HOLIDAY RECIPES

Our holiday best fills these pages with classic reader recipes, pretty pies, shortcut cakes, quick entrées, and food gifts galore.

SOUTHERN LIVING CHRISTMAS CLASSICS

Our readers share what makes each of these dishes Christmas classy. The recipes range from savory to sweet and will have instant success at your holiday table.

FOR ENTERTAINING

Drizzle Pecan Sticks with melted chocolate or white chocolate (we tested with 4 ounces of Ghirardelli candy coating). Let cookies stand 30 minutes for drizzle to harden. Serve cookies with ice cream in goblets or with coffee.

Pecan Sticks

PECAN STICKS `Make Ahead`

Lisa Reid O'Rourke of Baton Rouge, Louisiana, shares her holiday secret—cook as much as you can in advance. Her philosophy works well for her big annual holiday gathering. "I invite all my friends," she says. "I start a couple of weeks before the occasion so I will have as few things as possible to do close to the party."

1   cup butter or margarine, softened
1   cup sugar
1   large egg, separated
2   cups all-purpose flour
1   teaspoon ground cinnamon
1   teaspoon ground nutmeg
1   teaspoon vanilla extract
¼   teaspoon salt
1¼   cups chopped pecans

Beat butter and sugar at medium speed with an electric mixer until creamy; add egg yolk, flour, and next 4 ingredients, beating well. Press dough evenly into a lightly greased 15" x 10" jellyroll pan.

Butter Coconut Pie

Beat egg white until soft peaks form; spread over dough in pan. Sprinkle with chopped pecans, gently pressing into dough.

Bake at 325° for 26 to 28 minutes. Cut into 2" x 1" sticks while warm. Cool on wire racks. Store in an airtight container up to 2 weeks or freeze up to 3 months. Yield: about 5 dozen.

Lisa Reid O'Rourke
Baton Rouge, Louisiana

Note: *For bigger cookies, cut Pecan Sticks into 3" x 1" bars. The yield will be about 4 dozen.*

BUTTER COCONUT PIE

For Yolanda Powers of Decatur, Alabama, the best gifts come from the heart—and her kitchen. When her four kids were young, she began baking cakes and pies for gifts. Yolanda attributes her baking passion to growing up in a family of great cooks. This coconut pie makes a nice gift packaged right in the disposable pan it's baked in.

1   (9") frozen deep-dish pastry shell (we tested with Mrs. Smith's)
1   cup sugar
1   tablespoon all-purpose flour
3   large eggs, lightly beaten
1   (3.5-ounce) can sweetened flaked coconut
½   cup evaporated milk
⅓   cup butter or margarine, melted
1   teaspoon vanilla extract

Line piecrust with parchment paper; fill with pie weights or dried beans. Bake at 400° for 10 minutes or until crust is lightly browned. Remove paper and weights.

Combine sugar and flour in a large bowl; stir in eggs. Add coconut and remaining 3 ingredients, stirring well. Pour filling into prepared piecrust. Bake at 325° for 35 to 40 minutes or until pie is set. Yield: 1 (9") pie.

Note: *You can use half a 15-ounce package of refrigerated piecrusts and a 9" pieplate instead of a frozen piecrust. The filling will be more shallow and crust may need shielding to prevent overbrowning.*

Yolanda Powers
Decatur, Alabama

CREAM CHEESE POUND CAKE

*Another one of Yolanda Powers's favorite desserts, this
delicately crumbed cake received the highest rating from our
staff, too. Cream cheese adds volume and contributes to the
rich, dense texture. One tip: Don't beat this cake batter as
long as you would for most pound cakes, or it'll rise out of
your pan.*

1½ cups butter, softened
1   (8-ounce) package cream cheese, softened
3   cups sugar
6   large eggs
3   cups all-purpose flour
⅛   teaspoon salt
1   tablespoon vanilla extract
Powdered sugar (optional)

Beat butter and cream cheese at medium speed with an
electric mixer about 30 seconds or until creamy. Gradually
add 3 cups sugar, beating 1 minute. Add eggs, 1 at a time,
beating just until yellow disappears. Combine flour and
salt; gradually add to butter mixture, beating at low speed
just until blended. Stir in vanilla. Spoon batter into a
greased and floured 10" tube or Bundt pan.

Bake at 300° for 1 hour and 30 to 40 minutes or until a
long wooden pick inserted in center comes out almost
clean. Cool in pan on a wire rack 10 to 15 minutes; remove
from pan, and cool completely on wire rack. Sprinkle with
powdered sugar, if desired. Yield: 1 (10") cake.

Yolanda Powers
Decatur, Alabama

Cappuccino Pound Cake: *Dissolve 3 tablespoons instant
espresso powder in 3 tablespoons hot water; add to batter along
with eggs.*

Triple Chocolate Clusters

Make Ahead • Quick & Easy

Here's another of Lisa Reid O'Rourke's scrumptious holiday recipes. This one's great for gift giving.

2   (4-ounce) white chocolate bars (we tested with Ghirardelli)
1   cup (6 ounces) milk chocolate morsels
1   cup (6 ounces) semisweet chocolate morsels
1½ cups chopped pecans
1½ cups broken pretzels

Melt first 3 ingredients in a heavy saucepan over low heat, stirring constantly. Stir in pecans and pretzels. Drop by heaping tablespoonfuls onto lightly greased wax paper. Chill in refrigerator at least 1 hour. Store in an airtight container in refrigerator up to 1 month. Yield: about 3 dozen.

Note: *For a firmer candy, use 3 cups semisweet chocolate morsels instead of the 3 types of chocolate.*

Lisa Reid O'Rourke
Baton Rouge, Louisiana

Triple Chocolate Clusters

SPINACH-PECAN SALAD   Quick & Easy

Kathy Moss's family challenged each other to bring some new dishes to the holiday feast one year, and this salad was her contribution. It was a big hit, as she recalls. "No one in the family had ever thought of spinach for the holiday meal!"

1	tablespoon butter or margarine
1	tablespoon light brown sugar
½	cup pecan halves
1	(7-ounce) package fresh baby spinach, washed
1	large Granny Smith apple, thinly sliced
½	cup crumbled blue cheese
3	tablespoons olive oil
2	tablespoons white vinegar
⅛	teaspoon salt
⅛	teaspoon pepper

Melt butter and sugar in a small skillet over low heat, stirring constantly. Add pecan halves; cook 2 to 3 minutes, turning to coat. Remove coated pecans from skillet, and cool on wax paper.

Toss spinach, apple, cheese, and pecans in a serving bowl. Whisk oil, vinegar, salt, and pepper; drizzle over salad, tossing gently to coat. Yield: 4 servings.

Kathy Moss
Siloam Springs, Arkansas

Spinach-Pecan Salad

Carrot Soufflé

CURRY-ALMOND CHEESE SPREAD

`Make Ahead`

West Virginians Robin Jean Davis and Scott Segal decided on a whim to treat their friends to a Christmas party. That was nine years ago. The formal event was such a success, the couple has been holding the annual get-together in their Charleston home ever since. Here they share one of their family's favorite recipes enjoyed at the annual event.

2   (8-ounce) packages cream cheese, softened
1   (9-ounce) jar mango chutney
1   cup slivered almonds, toasted
1   tablespoon curry powder
½   teaspoon dry mustard
Toasted slivered almonds

Process first 5 ingredients in a food processor until smooth, stopping to scrape down sides. Cover and chill spread 1 hour.

Spoon spread into a crock; chill until ready to serve. Sprinkle with almonds just before serving. Serve with crackers, celery sticks, and endive leaves. Yield: 3 cups.

Robin Jean Davis and Scott Segal
Charleston, West Virginia

CARROT SOUFFLÉ

"I love carrots," says Trish Conroy. "They're great as a side dish." This old-fashioned bake, she says, has become a family favorite.

1   pound carrots, peeled and chopped
3   large eggs, lightly beaten
½   cup sugar
½   cup butter or margarine, melted
3   tablespoons all-purpose flour
1   teaspoon baking powder
1   teaspoon vanilla extract

Cook carrot in boiling water to cover 45 minutes or until very tender. Drain.

Process carrot in a food processor until smooth, stopping to scrape down sides.

Stir together carrot purée, eggs, and remaining ingredients. Spoon into a lightly greased 1-quart baking dish. Bake at 350° for 45 minutes or until set. Yield: 6 servings.

Trish Conroy
Lynchburg, Virginia

Curry-Almond Cheese Spread

EASY AS PIE

From main-dish to dessert, these pies offer plenty of diversity. Find a trio of savory pies plus familiar holiday sweets with some shortcuts woven in.

Cinnamon Mocha Pie

CINNAMON MOCHA PIE

You'll get a big cinnamon surprise when you bite into this dense, fudgy chocolate pie.

½ cup butter or margarine
1 tablespoon instant coffee granules
4 (1-ounce) unsweetened chocolate squares
3 large eggs
1 cup sugar
1 teaspoon vanilla extract
⅓ cup all-purpose flour
1 tablespoon ground cinnamon
1 (9") frozen deep-dish pastry shell
Unsweetened whipped cream
Ground cinnamon

Melt butter in a small saucepan over medium-low heat. Stir in coffee granules. Add chocolate, stirring until melted. Remove from heat. Cool slightly.

Beat eggs with a wire whisk; gradually beat in sugar. Slowly stir in cooled, melted chocolate mixture and vanilla. Stir in flour and 1 tablespoon cinnamon. Pour filling into pastry shell.

Bake at 350° for 25 minutes or until set. Serve slightly warm or at room temperature with whipped cream and more cinnamon. Yield: 1 (9") pie.

Note: *For added indulgence, drizzle some caramel topping over each serving.*

PUMPKIN CREAM PIE

Make Ahead

Gingersnaps and pumpkin are a divine match in this make-ahead holiday dessert. It's good chilled or frozen.

25 (2") gingersnap cookies, finely crushed (we tested with Murray's)

¼ cup butter or margarine, melted

1 (8-ounce) package cream cheese, softened

1 (15-ounce) can pumpkin

1 teaspoon ground cinnamon

½ teaspoon ground allspice

½ teaspoon ground ginger

¼ teaspoon ground nutmeg

½ cup heavy whipping cream

1½ cups powdered sugar

Garnishes: sweetened whipped cream, gingersnap cookies

Stir together crushed gingersnaps and butter; press into a greased 9" pieplate. Bake at 350° for 8 minutes. Cool completely on a wire rack.

Beat cream cheese in a large bowl at medium speed with an electric mixer until creamy. Add pumpkin and next 4 ingredients; beat until blended.

Beat whipping cream until foamy; gradually add powdered sugar, beating until stiff peaks form. (Mixture will be very thick.) Fold whipped cream into pumpkin filling until blended. Spoon into crust. Cover and chill pie at least 8 hours. Garnish, if desired. Yield: 1 (9") pie.

Frozen White Chocolate-Mint Pie

FROZEN WHITE CHOCOLATE-MINT PIE

Frosty slices of this white chocolate and peppermint pie are wrapped in a dark chocolate cookie crust for contrast.

3 (4-ounce) white chocolate bars, divided (we tested with Ghirardelli)

2 large eggs, beaten

⅓ cup powdered sugar

1¾ cups heavy whipping cream, divided

2 to 3 teaspoons peppermint extract

1 teaspoon vanilla extract

1 (6-ounce) chocolate crumb crust

8 chocolate wafer cookies

Place 2 chocolate bars in top of a double boiler over a pan of simmering water; stir until chocolate melts.

Stir a small amount of chocolate into beaten eggs; add to remaining chocolate, stirring constantly. Stir in powdered sugar and ¼ cup whipping cream until smooth. Cook over medium heat, stirring constantly, until a candy thermometer registers 160°. Remove from heat; cool, stirring constantly. Stir in flavorings.

Beat remaining 1½ cups whipping cream at high speed with an electric mixer until stiff peaks form. Gently fold whipped cream into chocolate. Spoon filling into crust, mounding in center.

Break 6 wafer cookies in half; place, cut sides down, into filling around edge of pie. Finely crush remaining 2 cookies; sprinkle crumbs over pie. Shave edges of remaining chocolate bar with a vegetable peeler to make white chocolate curls. Sprinkle curls over pie. Cover and freeze pie at least 8 hours. Yield: 1 (9") pie.

Pumpkin Cream Pie

MAPLE PENUCHE PIE

This rich pie gets its inspiration from the creamy fudgelike candy (penuche) made with brown sugar and butter.

½ (15-ounce) package refrigerated piecrusts
4 large eggs
1 cup firmly packed light brown sugar
1 cup light corn syrup
¼ cup butter, melted
2 teaspoons maple flavoring
¼ teaspoon salt
1¼ cups coarsely chopped walnuts

Fit piecrust into a 9" pieplate according to package directions; fold edges under, and crimp.

Whisk together eggs and next 5 ingredients; stir in nuts. Pour into prepared piecrust.

Bake at 350° for 55 minutes or until pie is set, shielding edges with aluminum foil after 45 minutes to prevent excessive browning. Cool completely on a wire rack. Yield: 1 (9") pie.

FOR ENTERTAINING

Use the other half of the package of refrigerated piecrusts for garnishes. Cut out pastry leaves using a leaf-shaped cookie cutter. Place leaves on an ungreased baking sheet. Bake at 350° for 10 minutes or until golden. Place pastry leaves on top of baked pie.

IRON SKILLET PIZZA PIE

You'll get 4 main-dish servings from this deep-dish pizza with a peppery crust. Using rotisserie chicken shortens your work time.

1 (7-ounce) jar roasted sweet red peppers, drained
¼ teaspoon salt
¼ teaspoon pepper
1 tablespoon olive oil
5 cups loosely packed fresh spinach leaves
1 teaspoon minced garlic
1 tablespoon yellow cornmeal
2 (10-ounce) cans refrigerated pizza dough
¼ teaspoon pepper, divided
¼ cup shredded Parmesan cheese, divided
1½ cups shredded rotisserie chicken
1 cup (4 ounces) shredded fontina cheese

Process roasted red peppers, ¼ teaspoon salt, and ¼ teaspoon pepper in a food processor until smooth.

Heat 1 tablespoon oil in a large nonstick skillet over medium heat until hot; add spinach and garlic, and cook 2 minutes or until spinach wilts. Set aside.

Maple Penuche Pie

Sprinkle cornmeal in bottom of a 10" cast-iron skillet. Roll each portion of dough into a 9" circle, rolling ⅛ teaspoon pepper and 2 tablespoons Parmesan cheese into each crust. Place 1 circle in skillet. Spread half of pureed pepper sauce over dough. Arrange spinach on top of sauce; top with chicken and fontina cheese. Drizzle with remaining half of pepper sauce. Top with remaining dough, cheese side up. Press crusts together to seal.

Bake at 400° for 23 minutes or until lightly browned. Let stand 5 minutes before serving. Yield: 1 (9") pie.

SHEPHERD'S PIE WITH HERBED MASHED POTATOES

Mushrooms and tender chunks of steak fill this potato-topped pie with goodness. A quick potato product and ready-made piecrust serve as tasty shortcuts.

2   tablespoons all-purpose flour
¼   teaspoon salt
¼   teaspoon pepper
¾   pound top round steak, cut into 1" pieces
2   tablespoons butter or margarine, melted
1½   cups sliced fresh mushrooms
1   large garlic clove, thinly sliced
1   (14.5-ounce) can petite diced tomatoes, drained (we tested with Hunt's)
1   (10-ounce) can French onion soup, undiluted
⅓   cup dry red wine
¼   teaspoon dried thyme
1   bay leaf
½   (15-ounce) package refrigerated piecrusts
1   (1-pound, 4-ounce) package country-style refrigerated mashed potatoes (we tested with Simply Potatoes)
1   teaspoon minced fresh rosemary
1   tablespoon butter or margarine, melted

Combine first 3 ingredients in a bowl. Add beef; toss to coat. Shake excess flour from beef, reserving excess flour in bowl. Brown beef in 2 tablespoons butter in a Dutch oven over medium-high heat 3 minutes. Stir in mushrooms, and cook 3 minutes. Stir in garlic, and cook 30 seconds. Remove from heat.

Add tomatoes and next 3 ingredients to reserved flour, stirring until flour dissolves; stir into meat. Add bay leaf. Bring to a boil, stirring to loosen particles from bottom of pan. Cover, reduce heat to low, and cook 1 hour and 45 minutes, stirring occasionally. Uncover, increase heat to medium-high, and cook 5 minutes or until thickened, stirring often. Remove from heat; discard bay leaf. Cover and keep meat filling warm.

Fit piecrust into a 9" pieplate according to package directions; fold edges under, and crimp.

Place potatoes in a microwave-safe bowl; stir in rosemary. Microwave at HIGH 4 minutes or until hot. Pour warm meat filling into pastry. Dollop potatoes over filling; spread over filling, sealing to edge of pastry. Drizzle with 1 tablespoon butter.

Bake, uncovered, at 450° for 10 minutes. Reduce oven temperature to 375°; bake 15 more minutes or until browned. Let stand 15 minutes before serving. Yield: 1 (9") pie.

Note: *Using homemade mashed potatoes instead of the refrigerated variety would make this main-dish pie even better.*

BACON, LEEK, AND GRUYÈRE QUICHE

Pair this creamy cheese quiche with a crisp green salad for a simple lunch or supper. It makes a nice brunch entrée, too.

4   bacon slices
2½   cups sliced leeks (about 3 medium)
1   large garlic clove, minced
1   (9") frozen deep-dish pastry shell
1½   cups (6 ounces) shredded Gruyère cheese, divided
5   large eggs, beaten
1   cup whipping cream
½   teaspoon freshly ground pepper
¼   teaspoon salt
Dash of ground nutmeg

Cook bacon in a large skillet until crisp; remove bacon and drain on paper towels, reserving drippings in skillet. Crumble bacon, and set aside.

Sauté leeks and garlic in drippings over medium heat 6 to 8 minutes or until tender.

Place pastry shell on a baking sheet. Sprinkle ¾ cup cheese in bottom of shell; sprinkle sautéed leeks and bacon over cheese.

Combine eggs and remaining 4 ingredients, stirring well. Pour into shell; sprinkle with remaining ¾ cup cheese.

Bake at 375° for 40 to 45 minutes or until set, shielding edges with aluminum foil after 30 minutes to prevent excessive browning. Let stand 5 minutes before serving. Yield: 1 (9") quiche.

ENTRÉES IN UNDER 30 MINUTES

Here are a half dozen hearty recipes ready in record time. Give yourself some of these great-tasting dinner gifts during the holiday rush.

Chicken Pizza with Arugula

CHICKEN PIZZA WITH ARUGULA

Quick & Easy
Total Time • 29 minutes

Try this quick pizza meal with upscale flavor. Pick up a hot rotisserie chicken on the way home from work. We liked the garlic- and herb-flavored chicken on this pizza.

1 rotisserie chicken
1 (14-ounce) Italian bread shell (we tested with Boboli)
1 cup dried tomato pesto (we tested with Melissa's)
2 cups (8 ounces) shredded mozzarella cheese
4 cups loosely packed fresh arugula (about 4 bunches) or mixed gourmet greens
1 garlic clove, minced
1 tablespoon olive oil
1 tablespoon white wine vinegar
¼ teaspoon salt
⅛ teaspoon pepper

Remove meat from bone (this is easy to do while chicken is still warm); set aside.

Place bread shell on a baking sheet. Spread pesto evenly over bread shell. Top with chicken; sprinkle with cheese. Bake at 450° for 8 to 12 minutes or until thoroughly heated.

Meanwhile, tear arugula into bite-sized pieces, if desired. Combine arugula, garlic, and remaining 4 ingredients. Top pizza with arugula just before serving. Yield: 1 (12") pizza.

CHICKEN-FRIED STEAK WITH PEPPERY CREAM GRAVY

Quick & Easy
Total Time • 25 minutes

Here's a Southern classic—cube steak crisply coated in cracker crumbs and enhanced by thick white gravy.

1 egg white, beaten
2¾ cups milk, divided
20 saltine crackers, crushed
1 cup all-purpose flour, divided
2 teaspoons salt, divided
1 teaspoon freshly ground pepper, divided
1 teaspoon poultry seasoning
1 cup vegetable oil
6 cube steaks (about 1½ pounds)
1 tablespoon butter or margarine

Combine egg white and ¼ cup milk in a bowl.

Combine crushed crackers, ¾ cup flour, 1 teaspoon salt, ¼ teaspoon pepper, and poultry seasoning in a shallow dish.

Heat oil in a large skillet over medium-high heat until hot. Dip 3 steaks, 1 at a time, into egg white mixture; dredge in seasoned crumbs. Press to coat. Fry 4 minutes on each side or until golden. Remove to a wire rack set over a jellyroll pan. Keep warm in a 225° oven. Repeat procedure with remaining 3 steaks.

Carefully drain hot oil, reserving browned bits and 2 tablespoons drippings in skillet. Melt butter in drippings over medium heat. Whisk in remaining ¼ cup flour, remaining 1 teaspoon salt, and remaining ¾ teaspoon pepper. Gradually whisk in remaining 2½ cups milk; cook over medium heat, whisking constantly, 5 minutes or until thickened and bubbly. Serve steak and gravy with mashed potatoes. Yield: 6 servings.

MAPLE- AND PECAN-GLAZED PORK TENDERLOIN

Quick & Easy
Total Time • 22 minutes

This entrée boasts pork tenderloin smothered in a sweet glaze of maple syrup, stone-ground mustard, pecans, and bourbon.

2 (¾- to 1-pound) pork tenderloins
½ teaspoon salt
1 tablespoon butter or margarine
1 tablespoon vegetable oil
½ cup chopped pecans
½ cup maple syrup
2 tablespoons stone-ground mustard
2 tablespoons bourbon

Sprinkle tenderloins with salt. Heat butter and oil in a large oven-proof skillet over medium-high heat until hot. Add tenderloins, and cook 3 minutes on each side until browned.

Meanwhile, combine pecans, syrup, and mustard in a small saucepan. Bring to a boil; reduce heat, and simmer, uncovered, 3 minutes or until thick. Stir in bourbon. Spread sauce over tenderloins in skillet.

Bake at 450° for 12 to 15 minutes or until meat thermometer inserted into thickest portion registers 160°. Remove tenderloins to a serving platter. Cover with aluminum foil, and let rest 10 minutes. Slice and serve with sauce remaining in skillet. Yield: 6 servings.

Chicken-Fried Steak with Peppery Cream Gravy

ORANGE-SCENTED PORK CHOPS

Quick & Easy
Total Time • 27 minutes

Your senses will come alive when you take a bite of this straightforward dish. Vegetables are diced to speed cooking, and the pork cut lends itself to this quick braise method.

4   boneless pork loin chops (¾" thick)
½   teaspoon salt
½   teaspoon freshly ground pepper
2   tablespoons all-purpose flour
2   tablespoons olive oil
1   onion, diced
2   carrots, diced
2   celery ribs, diced
¾   cup fresh orange juice
¼   cup dry white wine
1   tablespoon grated orange rind
1   (3.2-ounce) bag quick-cooking rice
½   teaspoon salt
¼   teaspoon freshly ground pepper

Sprinkle both sides of pork with ½ teaspoon salt and ½ teaspoon pepper. Place flour in a shallow bowl; dredge pork in flour.

Heat olive oil in a large nonstick skillet over medium-high heat. Add pork, and cook 2 minutes on each side or just until browned. Remove pork from skillet. Add onion, carrot, and celery to skillet, and sauté 4 to 5 minutes or until almost tender. Add orange juice, wine, and rind to skillet; bring to a boil. Return pork to skillet. Cover, reduce heat, and simmer 3 to 4 minutes; turn pork, and simmer 3 to 4 more minutes or until tender.

Cook rice according to package directions. Drain, and set aside.

Remove pork from skillet, and keep warm. Simmer vegetables, uncovered, 4 to 5 more minutes or until liquid is reduced to about ¼ cup. Add rice, ½ teaspoon salt, and ¼ teaspoon pepper. Serve pork over rice. Yield: 4 servings.

SHRIMP IN GARLIC BUTTER

Quick & Easy
Total Time • 10 minutes

Lots of saucy garlic butter will make you want to sop up every dribble of this dish with crusty bread. Quick tip: Call ahead to your grocer to order shrimp that's already peeled and deveined. If you decide to peel and devein it yourself, purchase 1⅔ pounds shrimp in the shells.

¼   cup butter
4   garlic cloves, chopped
1¼ pounds peeled and deveined, large fresh shrimp
2   tablespoons fresh lemon juice (about 1 lemon)
2   tablespoons chopped fresh chives
½   teaspoon salt
¼   teaspoon pepper
Garnish: fresh chives

Melt butter in a large skillet over medium-high heat; add garlic, and cook 1 minute or until browned. Add shrimp, and cook, stirring often, 4 minutes or until shrimp turn pink. Stir in lemon juice and next 3 ingredients. Serve over rice or with crusty bread. Garnish, if desired. Yield: 2 to 3 servings.

Shrimp in Garlic Butter

Veal Chops with Rosemary and Olives

VEAL CHOPS WITH ROSEMARY AND OLIVES

Quick & Easy

Total Time • 24 minutes

Cracked green olives, fresh rosemary, and lemon juice add impeccable taste to this rich veal entrée.

2   (1½"-thick) bone-in veal rib chops
¼   teaspoon salt
¼   teaspoon freshly ground pepper
3   tablespoons butter or margarine, divided
2   garlic cloves, minced
⅓   cup cracked green olives, pitted and coarsely chopped
     (we tested with Peloponnese)
2   tablespoons fresh lemon juice
2   tablespoons water
1   tablespoon chopped fresh rosemary
Garnish: fresh rosemary

Sprinkle both sides of veal with salt and pepper. Melt 1 tablespoon butter in a large skillet over medium-high heat. Add veal, and cook 8 to 10 minutes on each side or to desired degree of doneness. Remove from skillet; cover and keep warm.

Reduce heat to medium; add garlic to skillet, and cook 30 seconds or until golden. Add olives, lemon juice, and water; cook 30 seconds, stirring to loosen particles from bottom of skillet. Add remaining 2 tablespoons butter, stirring just until butter melts. Return chops and any juices to skillet; cook 1 minute or until thoroughly heated. Sprinkle with rosemary, and serve immediately. Garnish, if desired. Yield: 2 servings.

Note: *An easy way to remove the pits from these partially cracked olives is to mash them with the flat side of a chef's knife.*

10 WAYS WITH TURKEY

The everpopular holiday bird leaves the platter for some delicious variations.
On these pages you'll find turkey versatility ranging from an elegant
rolled entrée to sassy sandwiches and a layered salad.

Spinach- and Herb-Stuffed
Turkey Roll

Spinach- and Herb-Stuffed Turkey Roll

Fresh thyme, oregano, and sage finesse the spinach and mushroom stuffing for this light entrée that makes a pretty presentation when sliced.

1 (8-ounce) package sliced fresh mushrooms, chopped
1 medium onion, finely chopped
2 garlic cloves, minced
1 tablespoon melted butter or olive oil
1 (10-ounce) package frozen chopped spinach, thawed and well drained
1 cup soft whole-wheat breadcrumbs (homemade)
⅓ cup refrigerated shredded Parmesan cheese
1 large egg, lightly beaten
1½ teaspoons chopped fresh thyme or ½ teaspoon dried thyme
1½ teaspoons chopped fresh oregano or ½ teaspoon dried oregano
½ teaspoon salt
½ teaspoon freshly ground pepper
1 (3- to 3½-pound) boneless turkey breast
1 teaspoon rubbed sage
1 teaspoon salt
½ teaspoon freshly ground pepper
¼ teaspoon paprika
1 tablespoon softened butter or olive oil
Garnishes: fresh thyme, sage, and oregano

Sauté first 3 ingredients in melted butter in a skillet over medium-high heat until onion is tender. Set aside.

Combine spinach and next 7 ingredients in a large bowl; stir in sautéed vegetables.

Remove and discard skin from turkey breast. Lay breast flat on heavy-duty plastic wrap (with what would have been skin side down). From center, slice horizontally, through thickest part of each side of breast almost to outer edge; flip cut piece and breast fillets over to enlarge breast. Top with more plastic wrap. Pound breast to flatten to ½" thickness.

Spread spinach filling over turkey breast, leaving a ½" border at sides. Roll up. Tie roll securely in several places with heavy string; place, seam side down, in a lightly greased shallow roasting pan.

Combine sage and next 3 ingredients. Rub softened butter over roll; rub with seasonings.

Bake, uncovered, at 350° for 1 hour and 10 minutes or until a meat thermometer registers 170°. Cover with aluminum foil, and let stand 15 minutes. Remove string and slice. Garnish, if desired. Yield: 8 servings.

Note: *An easy way to flatten boneless turkey breast is to place heavy-duty plastic wrap over the top and gently hit it with an empty wine bottle or a rolling pin to desired thickness.*

Note: *Some of our staff enjoyed this stuffed turkey breast as is, without gravy. Others suggested adding a gravy of choice. We liked the flavor and color of gravy using a 0.88-ounce package of turkey gravy mix (we tested with French's).*

Smoked Turkey Breast

Having a smoked turkey breast on hand during the holidays leads to sandwich perfection.

Hickory wood chunks
1 tablespoon garlic powder
1 tablespoon pepper
2 teaspoons salt
1 (5-pound) bone-in turkey breast
2 fresh rosemary sprigs

Soak wood chunks in water at least 1 hour.

Combine garlic powder, pepper, and salt in a small bowl. Rub a small amount of spice blend under skin of turkey; rub the remainder on outside of bird. Place rosemary sprigs under skin.

Prepare charcoal fire in smoker; let burn 15 to 20 minutes.

Drain wood chunks, and place on hot coals. Place water pan in smoker; add water to depth of fill line. Place turkey in center of lower food rack; cover with smoker lid.

Cook 5 to 6 hours or until a meat thermometer inserted into thickest portion registers 170°, adding additional water to depth of fill line, if necessary. Remove from smoker, and let stand 10 minutes before slicing. Yield: 6 to 8 servings.

Tip: *Use a digital probe thermometer to be sure turkey cooks to perfect doneness. Simply insert thermometer into thickest portion of bird, letting cord extend to outside of smoker. This eliminates loss of heat from the smoker, since you don't have to open the lid to check on the turkey's progress.*

LAYERED TURKEY AND CORNBREAD SALAD

The popular seven-layer salad takes a tasty twist with turkey and crumbled cornbread.

1   (15-ounce) jar roasted garlic dressing (we tested with Marzetti's)
¼   cup buttermilk
1   head romaine lettuce, shredded
2½ cups chopped smoked turkey (about 1 pound)
8   ounces crumbled feta cheese
1   (12-ounce) jar roasted sweet red peppers, drained and chopped
3   cups cornbread, crumbled
1   (12-ounce) package bacon, cooked and crumbled
5   green onions, chopped

Stir together dressing and buttermilk. Layer half each of lettuce and next 6 ingredients in a 4-quart glass bowl; top with half of dressing. Repeat layers with remaining ingredients, ending with dressing. Cover and chill at least 2 hours before serving. Yield: 6 to 8 servings.

Layered Turkey and Cornbread Salad

ULTIMATE ROASTED TURKEY ON THE LIGHT SIDE

Garlic, onion, and apple fill the turkey cavity with aromatic appeal, while a sage and poultry seasoning mix rubbed under the skin gives this roasted bird added pizzazz. You'd never guess this was a light recipe.

¾   cup apple cider
5   tablespoons dark corn syrup, divided
1   (12-pound) fresh or frozen turkey, thawed
1   tablespoon poultry seasoning
1   tablespoon rubbed sage
1   teaspoon salt
¼   teaspoon pepper
4   garlic cloves, sliced
4   onions, quartered
4   Golden Delicious apples, cored and quartered
1   teaspoon butter
1   (14-ounce) can low-sodium fat-free chicken broth
1   tablespoon cornstarch
Garnish: fresh sage

Combine cider and 4 tablespoons corn syrup in a small saucepan; bring to a boil. Remove from heat, and set aside.

Remove giblets and neck from turkey; reserve for making homemade broth. Rinse turkey with cold water; pat dry. Trim excess fat. Place turkey, breast side up, in a broiler pan coated with cooking spray. Lift wing tips up and over back; tuck under turkey.

Combine poultry seasoning, sage, salt, and pepper. Using fingers, carefully loosen skin from turkey at neck area, working down to breast and thigh area. Rub seasoning mixture under skin. Place half of garlic, 4 onion quarters, and 4 apple quarters into body cavity. Tie legs together with heavy string, or tuck them under flap of skin. Arrange remaining garlic, onion, and apple around turkey in pan.

Roast at 375° for 45 minutes. Baste turkey with reserved cider syrup; cover with aluminum foil. Bake 1½ more hours or until a meat thermometer inserted into meaty part of thigh registers 180°, basting turkey and vegetables with cider syrup 4 times at regular intervals.

While turkey bakes, melt butter in a medium saucepan over medium-high heat. Add reserved giblets and neck; sauté 2 minutes on each side or until browned. Add broth, and bring to a boil. Cover, reduce heat, and simmer 45 minutes. Pour broth through a wire mesh strainer into a bowl, discarding solids. Reserve broth.

Ultimate Roasted Turkey
on the Light Side

When turkey is done, carefully transfer it to a carving board, reserving drippings in pan for gravy. Transfer apple and onion quarters to a serving platter. Cover turkey with aluminum foil, and let rest 15 minutes before carving. Discard skin, if desired. Carve turkey, arranging slices on serving platter with onion and apple; keep warm.

Place a zip-top plastic bag inside a 2-cup glass measuring cup. Pour pan drippings through a wire mesh strainer into bag; let stand 10 minutes (fat will rise to top). Seal bag; carefully snip off 1 bottom corner of bag. Drain drippings back into broiler pan, stopping before fat layer reaches opening; discard fat.

Combine ¼ cup reserved broth and cornstarch, stirring well; add to remaining broth. Combine broth mixture, remaining 1 tablespoon corn syrup, and drippings in broiler pan or a large saucepan on stovetop over medium heat, stirring to loosen particles from bottom of pan. Bring to a boil; cook, whisking constantly, 1 minute or until slightly thickened. Serve gravy with turkey. (Gravy will be dark and thin.) Garnish, if desired. Yield: 12 servings.

Health Note: *Removing the skin before serving and discarding the fat from drippings help qualify this entrée as low fat. We chose to leave the turkey skin intact for a pretty presentation.*

TURKEY TALK

THAWING

For an average 9- to 12-pound bird, allow 2 to 3 days thawing time in the refrigerator (24 hours for every 5 pounds). Leave turkey in its original wrapper, and place in a pan to catch juices that drip. Once thawed, turkey should be baked right away.

STUFFING

Stuff turkey just before roasting, not the night before. And never refrigerate a cooked, stuffed turkey with stuffing intact. Remove stuffing promptly after baking and refrigerate any leftovers in a separate container. If you choose not to stuff a turkey, there are many options for infusing flavor into the meat as it cooks. You can cut up an onion, apple, orange, or celery ribs with leaves and insert them into turkey cavity, or tuck sprigs of fresh herbs into cavity.

CARVING

Use a sharp knife and a large cutting board (with a damp towel underneath to keep it from slipping). Carve from one side of turkey at a time, carving only as much meat as needed for serving. Grasp leg and pull away from body; cut through joint between thigh and body. Slice thigh (dark) meat. Cut through joint between wing and breast to release wing from bird. To slice breast without removing it, steady bird with carving fork and make a deep horizontal cut into breast just above wing. Beginning at outer top edge of breast, cut thin slices from the top down to the horizontal cut.

SERVING

A good rule of thumb to consider when you're buying your holiday bird and thinking about your guest list is a pound of meat per person. Then buy a slightly larger bird if you're counting on leftovers for sandwiches.

GARNISHING

Fresh herbs make a lovely evergreen garnish for the turkey platter. Rosemary, thyme, and sage are hearty herbs you'll find during winter, ideal for seasoning a turkey (tuck a sprig under the skin), as well as adorning the finished product. Lady apples, kumquats, baby artichokes and other baby vegetables, small onions, whole nuts in the shell, roasted vegetable chunks, and grape clusters are other options for the platter. And, of course, fresh parsley and kale are always available.

Turkey Hash

Here's what to do with that last bit of turkey leftover from the big feast. Top this turkey hash with poached eggs for a quick brunch idea.

1½ cups cubed unpeeled red potato
1 cup chopped onion
¼ teaspoon salt
¼ teaspoon freshly ground pepper
2 tablespoons vegetable oil
2 cups cubed cooked turkey
½ cup milk
2 tablespoons chopped fresh parsley
Freshly ground pepper

Combine first 4 ingredients.

Heat oil in a large nonstick skillet over medium-high heat until hot. Add potatoes and onion. Sauté 8 to 10 minutes. Add turkey, and cook 5 minutes or until potatoes are tender. Stir in milk. Cover and simmer 1 to 2 minutes. Remove from heat. Sprinkle with parsley and pepper. Serve with buttered grits or toast. Yield: 2 to 3 servings.

Turkey Hash

Turkey Tetrazzini

Tetrazzini is a timeless pasta dish rich in familiar flavors and family appeal. Roasted red pepper jazzes up this version.

1 onion, chopped
1 large green bell pepper, chopped
2 garlic cloves, minced
1 tablespoon vegetable oil
⅓ cup butter or margarine
⅓ cup all-purpose flour
3 cups half-and-half or milk
1 cup shredded Parmesan cheese
½ teaspoon salt
½ teaspoon pepper
7 ounces spaghetti, cooked
3 cups chopped cooked turkey
1 (7-ounce) jar roasted sweet red peppers, drained and chopped
1½ cups soft white or whole wheat breadcrumbs (homemade)
¾ cup shredded Parmesan cheese
2 tablespoons butter or margarine, melted

Sauté first 3 ingredients in hot oil in a large skillet over medium heat 5 minutes or until tender. Remove from heat, and set aside.

Melt ⅓ cup butter in a heavy saucepan over low heat. Whisk in flour until smooth. Cook, whisking constantly, 1 minute. Gradually whisk in half-and-half; cook over medium heat, whisking constantly, until thick and bubbly. Stir in 1 cup cheese, salt, and pepper.

Toss sautéed vegetables with cheese sauce, spaghetti, and turkey. Place chopped red peppers on paper towels to prevent the red color from bleeding into the casserole. Gently stir roasted pepper into spaghetti. Spoon into a greased 13" x 9" baking dish.

Combine breadcrumbs, ¾ cup cheese, and melted butter; sprinkle over casserole. Bake, uncovered, at 350° for 25 minutes or until breadcrumbs are toasted and casserole is thoroughly heated. Yield: 6 servings.

Note: *To make serving the casserole easier, break spaghetti in half before cooking. And be sure to salt the pasta water for flavor.*

Turkey-Artichoke Tartlets

TURKEY-ARTICHOKE TARTLETS Make Ahead

Turkey, marinated artichokes, pecans, and green onions fill these flaky finger foods.

1   (15-ounce) package refrigerated piecrusts
2   cups diced cooked turkey
2   (6½-ounce) jars marinated artichoke hearts, drained and chopped
⅔   cup coarsely chopped pecans, toasted
¼   cup minced green onions
3   tablespoons mayonnaise
3   tablespoons sour cream
1   garlic clove, minced
½   teaspoon salt
½   teaspoon ground black pepper
¼   teaspoon ground red pepper
Garnish: celery leaves

Unfold 1 piecrust, and press out fold lines; cut with a 2½" round cutter. Press rounds into 1¾" miniature muffin pans, trimming edges as needed. Repeat procedure with remaining piecrust, rerolling and cutting dough scraps.

Bake at 425° for 7 minutes or until shells are golden brown. Remove tart shells from pans, and cool on wire racks.

Meanwhile, stir together turkey and next 9 ingredients; spoon evenly into tart shells. Garnish, if desired. Yield: 3½ dozen.

Make Ahead: *Bake tart shells and store overnight in zip-top plastic bags. Prepare turkey filling and store in refrigerator. Assemble just before serving.*

Use a tart tamper to help press dough evenly into mini muffin pans.

Spicy Fried Turkey Breast

Fried turkey has become quite the rage in recent years; maybe it's because of the ultracrispy coating and juicy meat so akin to a good bite of fried chicken. See our tips below for safe operation.

1   (5- to 6-pound) bone-in turkey breast, thawed
1   quart water
2   tablespoons salt
2   teaspoons garlic salt
2   teaspoons ground red pepper
1   teaspoon ground black pepper
1   cup all-purpose flour
1   teaspoon salt
1   teaspoon ground black pepper
½   teaspoon garlic salt
½   teaspoon ground red pepper
1   to 1½ gallons peanut oil

- *Always fry a turkey outdoors on flat concrete—never indoors, in a garage, on a wooden deck, or on an unstable surface.*
- *Fry turkey away from buildings and anything flammable.*
- *Oil will expand in the cooker once you add the turkey; never fill cooker with oil past the oil fill line.*
- *Use the thermometer provided with the fryer. Don't heat oil above the temperature recommended by the manufacturer. Use peanut oil for frying because it cooks at higher temperatures than other oils without smoking.*
- *Drain all juices from turkey, and thoroughly pat turkey dry before frying. Interior juices can cause hot oil to bubble over.*
- *If turkey's been frozen, be sure it's totally thawed and drained before lowering it into the hot oil.*
- *Never leave fryer unattended. Keep children and pets away from fryer when in use.*
- *Don't move fryer during operation or while oil is hot.*
- *Use well-insulated oven mitts when touching pot or handles. Wear safety goggles to protect your eyes from oil splatter.*
- *Wear a long sleeve shirt and long pants when lowering and raising turkey from oil.*
- *You may want to enlist a friend to hold one end of a long broom handle while you hold the other end to lower turkey on fryer rod into hot oil. This keeps you safely away from spatters.*

Rinse turkey with cold water; pat dry. Combine 1 quart water and next 4 ingredients in a large bowl. Place turkey breast, breast side down, in marinade. Cover and marinate in refrigerator at least 8 hours or up to 24 hours.

Thoroughly drain, but don't rinse turkey; discard marinade.

Combine flour and next 4 ingredients in a large bowl. Dredge turkey in seasoned flour, pressing gently to coat, and let stand 10 minutes. (This helps the coating adhere during frying.)

Pour peanut oil to fill line into a deep propane turkey fryer, and heat to 325°.

Place turkey on fryer rod. Wearing heavy-duty work gloves or an oven mitt, carefully lower turkey into hot oil using rod attachment. Slowly increase heat so oil temperature returns to 325° to 350° (this may take some time). Fry turkey 40 minutes or until a meat thermometer inserted in meaty part of breast registers 170°. Remove from oil; drain and cool slightly before serving. Yield: 6 servings.

Smoked Turkey Wraps

Caramelized onions fill these wraps with mellow goodness and are the perfect partner for smoked turkey, bacon, and garlicky herb cheese.

1   (6.5-ounce) package garlic-and-herb spreadable cheese (we tested with Alouette)
4   (9" or 10") flour tortillas
Caramelized Onions (recipe at right)
1   pound thinly sliced smoked turkey
8   bacon slices, cooked and crumbled
2   cups loosely packed baby spinach or gourmet mixed salad greens

Spread cheese evenly over tortillas, leaving a ½" border around edges. Top with Caramelized Onions, turkey, bacon, and spinach.

Roll up tortillas; wrap in parchment paper. Chill. Cut each wrap in half diagonally, and secure with wooden picks, if necessary. Yield: 4 servings.

Make Ahead: *If you'd like to prepare the wraps up to 24 hours ahead, wrap them in parchment paper, and then in plastic wrap to keep them from drying out. Chill until ready to serve.*

Shortcut Solution: *Buy and use already cooked real bacon.*

Smoked Turkey Wrap

CARAMELIZED ONIONS

2   tablespoons olive oil
2   large sweet onions, chopped
1   tablespoon sugar
2   teaspoons balsamic vinegar
¼   teaspoon freshly ground pepper

Heat oil in a large skillet over medium heat; add onions and sugar. Cook, stirring often, 30 to 35 minutes or until caramelized. Stir in vinegar and pepper. Remove from heat, and cool completely. Yield: about 1 cup.

TURKEY BURGERS WITH CRANBERRY KETCHUP

An innovative homemade ketchup dresses up these well-seasoned, pan-seared turkey burgers.

1   pound ground turkey (white and dark meat)
½   cup wheat germ
1   small onion, diced
2   garlic cloves, minced
1   teaspoon dried oregano
½   teaspoon salt
½   teaspoon pepper
½   teaspoon fennel seeds, crushed
1   tablespoon vegetable oil
4   onion hamburger buns
Cranberry Ketchup
Mayonnaise
Green leaf lettuce leaves

Combine first 8 ingredients in a large bowl; shape into 4 ½"-thick patties. Pour oil into a large nonstick skillet. Place over medium-high heat until hot. Add patties, and cook 3 minutes on each side or until done. Serve on onion buns with Cranberry Ketchup, mayonnaise, and lettuce leaves. Yield: 4 servings.

CRANBERRY KETCHUP

1   (16-ounce) can whole-berry cranberry sauce
½   cup sugar
⅓   cup apple cider vinegar
½   teaspoon ground cinnamon
¼   teaspoon salt
¼   teaspoon pepper
¼   teaspoon ground allspice

Combine all ingredients in a saucepan. Bring to a boil; reduce heat, and simmer, uncovered, 10 minutes or until slightly thickened, stirring often. Store in an airtight container in refrigerator up to 2 weeks. Yield: about 2 cups.

FOR ENTERTAINING

Serve Cranberry Ketchup over cream cheese with gingersnaps or wheat crackers as a party appetizer.

Turkey Burger with Cranberry Ketchup

SHORTCUT CAKES

*These recipes take the cake. Each has one or more secret ingredients
to give you a jump start for dessert. Graciously accept praise—
no one needs to know you didn't spend all day baking.*

**Streusel-Sour Cream
Coffee Cake**

STREUSEL-SOUR CREAM COFFEE CAKE `Make Ahead`

A streak of chocolaty-toffee streusel in the center and on top of this easy sheet cake make it to-die-for. It's a make-ahead coffee cake that's perfect for Christmas morning.

1   (26.5-ounce) package cinnamon streusel coffee cake mix (we tested with Pillsbury)
3   large eggs
1   cup sour cream
⅓   cup butter or margarine, softened
¼   cup water
1   teaspoon vanilla extract
8   (1.4-ounce) chocolate-covered toffee bars, chopped (we tested with Skor bars)
1   cup chopped pecans, toasted
⅓   cup uncooked regular oats

Beat coffee cake mix and next 5 ingredients in a large mixing bowl at low speed with an electric mixer 1 minute or just until dry ingredients are moistened. Beat at medium speed 2 minutes. Spread half of batter into a greased and floured 13" x 9" pan.

Combine streusel packet, candy, pecans, and oats; sprinkle half of streusel topping over batter in pan. Dollop and then spread remaining batter over streusel layer. Sprinkle with remaining streusel topping. Bake at 350° for 40 minutes. Cool in pan on a wire rack. Drizzle glaze packet over top of cake. Yield: 15 servings.

COCONUT-ALMOND TOFFEE CAKE

Simple cake mix becomes a thick, rich batter when laden with toffee bits, almonds, and coconut. Wait'll you taste the results.

1   (18.25-ounce) package yellow cake mix (we tested with Betty Crocker Supermoist with pudding)
4   large eggs
1   (8-ounce) carton sour cream
¼   cup vegetable oil
1   teaspoon almond extract
1   (10-ounce) package almond toffee bits (we tested with Hershey's Heath Bits O' Brickle)
½   cup chopped almonds
½   cup sweetened flaked coconut
1   cup sifted powdered sugar
3   tablespoons half-and-half
¼   cup sweetened flaked coconut, toasted
¼   cup sliced almonds, toasted

Beat first 5 ingredients at medium speed with an electric mixer 2 minutes or until blended. Fold in toffee bits, chopped almonds, and ½ cup coconut. (Batter will be thick.) Spoon batter into a greased and floured 12-cup Bundt pan.

Bake at 350° for 42 to 45 minutes or until a long wooden pick inserted in center comes out clean. Cool cake in pan on a wire rack 10 minutes; remove cake from pan, and place on wire rack.

Combine powdered sugar and half-and-half; drizzle over warm cake. Sprinkle with toasted coconut and almonds. Yield: 1 (10") cake.

CHOCOLATE CHIP COOKIE CHEESECAKE `Make Ahead`

Once you stir in a few extra goodies, a no-bake cheesecake and storebought cookies become a dessert both kids and adults will like. Be sure to use firm chocolate chip cookies rather than the soft kind. We liked the texture they added.

1   (11.1-ounce) package no-bake cheesecake dessert (we tested with Jell-O)
⅓   cup chocolate cookie crumbs (we tested with chocolate teddy bear-shaped cookies)
½   cup butter or margarine, melted
14   chocolate chip cookies (we tested with Chips Ahoy)
¼   cup fudge sauce
1½   cups cold milk
1   (3-ounce) package cream cheese, softened
1½   cups frozen whipped topping, thawed
2   tablespoons fudge sauce

Prepare crust for cheesecake according to package directions, adding chocolate cookie crumbs and melted butter. Press into a 9" pieplate.

Arrange 8 cookies in a single layer in crust; drizzle with ¼ cup fudge sauce.

Prepare filling according to package directions, using 1½ cups milk and beating in softened cream cheese; spoon into crust. Cover and chill 8 hours.

Spread whipped topping over filling. Chop remaining 6 cookies; sprinkle over whipped topping. Drizzle with 2 tablespoons fudge sauce. Chill until ready to serve. Yield: 1 (9") cheesecake.

Christmas Cupcakes

CHRISTMAS CUPCAKES

Cake mix and canned frosting turn into some of the best cupcakes around once you add the surprise cream cheese-and-chocolate chip filling. Decorator sprinkles create festive magic on top. We really liked these chocolate cupcakes plain, too.

2   (3-ounce) packages cream cheese, softened
½   cup sugar
1   large egg
1   cup (6 ounces) milk chocolate morsels
1   (18.25-ounce) package Swiss chocolate cake mix or devil's food cake mix (we tested with Duncan Hines)
1   (16-ounce) container homestyle creamy vanilla frosting
1   (16-ounce) container chocolate fudge frosting
Decorator sprinkles (optional)

Beat cream cheese at medium speed with an electric mixer until smooth; add sugar, beating well. Add egg, beating just until blended. Stir in chocolate morsels.

Prepare cake mix according to package directions. Place baking cups in muffin pans. Spoon batter into cups, filling two-thirds full.

Spoon a scant tablespoonful cream cheese mixture in center of each cupcake. Bake at 350° for 19 to 21 minutes or until a wooden pick inserted off center comes out clean. Cool in pans on wire racks 5 minutes. Remove from pans, and cool completely on wire racks.

Frost cupcakes with desired flavor frosting. Or swirl frostings together with a knife or thin metal spatula, if desired (see photo below). Top with decorator sprinkles, if desired. Yield: 2½ dozen.

Swirled frostings adorn this cake for adults.

Holiday candy sprinkles claim this cake for kids.

HOLIDAY LANE CAKE

We've made this fancy Southern cake doable for anybody. The shortcut? Cake mix and frosting mix. You're just in charge of the gooey filling and baking the cake, of course.

1   (18.25-ounce) package white cake mix (we tested with Duncan Hines)
3   large eggs
1¼   cups milk
¼   cup vegetable oil
Raisin-Nut Filling
1   (7.2-ounce) package fluffy white frosting mix (we tested with Betty Crocker)
½   cup boiling water
Garnish: maraschino cherries with stems

Beat first 4 ingredients at medium speed with an electric mixer 2 minutes. Pour batter into 3 greased and floured 8" round cakepans. Bake at 350° for 15 to 20 minutes or until a wooden pick inserted in center comes out clean. Cool in pans on wire racks 10 minutes; remove from pans, and cool on wire racks. Wrap cake layers in nonstick aluminum foil, and freeze 30 minutes. (This step aids in frosting the finished product.)

Unwrap layers. Spread Raisin-Nut Filling between layers, reserving about 1⅓ cups for top of cake.

Beat frosting mix and ½ cup boiling water at low speed 30 seconds. Scrape down sides of bowl; beat at high speed 5 to 7 minutes or until stiff peaks form. Spread frosting on sides of cake. Spread reserved filling on top of cake. Let stand at least 1 hour before serving. Garnish, if desired. Yield: 1 (3-layer) cake.

RAISIN-NUT FILLING

½   cup butter
1   cup sugar
8   egg yolks
1   cup chopped pecans, toasted
1   cup raisins
1   cup sweetened flaked coconut
¾   cup halved maraschino cherries, drained
¼   cup bourbon or orange juice
1   teaspoon vanilla extract

Melt butter in a heavy saucepan over medium heat. Stir together sugar and egg yolks, and stir into butter. Cook, stirring constantly, 12 to 14 minutes or until thickened. Remove from heat; stir in pecans and remaining ingredients. Cool to room temperature. Yield: about 3½ cups.

SAVANNAH CHRISTMAS PRALINE-SPICE CAKE

Two ingredients dress up canned frosting for this decadent layer cake. We offer you a double dose of candied nut garnishes, too. If you'd like to simplify, just choose one.

1   (18-ounce) package carrot cake mix (we tested with Betty Crocker)
3   large eggs
1   cup water
⅓   cup vegetable oil
3   large carrots, grated
2   cups chopped pecans, toasted and divided
1   (8-ounce) can crushed pineapple, well drained
⅔   cup sugar
24 pecan halves
2   (16-ounce) containers homestyle cream cheese frosting (we tested with Duncan Hines)
1   tablespoon vanilla extract
Praline Crumbles

Grease 3 (8") round cakepans. Line with wax paper; grease wax paper. Set aside.

Beat first 4 ingredients at low speed with an electric mixer 30 seconds. Beat at medium speed 2 minutes. Stir in carrot, 1 cup pecans, and pineapple. Pour batter evenly into pans.

Bake at 350° for 20 to 22 minutes or until a wooden pick inserted in center comes out clean. Cool in pans on wire racks 10 minutes. Remove from pans, and cool completely on wire racks. Wrap cake layers in nonstick aluminum foil. Freeze 30 minutes. (This step aids in frosting the finished product.)

Coat a sheet of wax paper with cooking spray; set aside.

Place sugar in a large heavy skillet. Cook over medium heat, stirring constantly with a wooden spoon, 5 to 10 minutes or until sugar melts and turns light brown. Remove from heat. Working quickly, drop pecan halves, a few at a time, into caramelized sugar, turning to coat. Using a fork, remove pecans to greased wax paper. Cool completely; remove from wax paper, and reserve for garnish.

Combine frosting, vanilla, and remaining 1 cup pecans in a bowl. Unwrap layers, and spread frosting between layers and on top and sides of cake. Let cake stand 1 hour before serving. Sprinkle Praline Crumbles over top of cake, and garnish rim of cake with candied pecans. Yield: 1 (3-layer) cake.

Note: *You can substitute 1 (18.25-ounce) package spice cake mix for the carrot cake mix, if you'd like. Increase the water to 1⅓ cups.*

PRALINE CRUMBLES

1   tablespoon butter
¼   cup sugar
½   cup chopped pecans

Melt butter in a medium skillet over low heat. Add sugar, reduce heat to medium-low, and cook until sugar melts. Stir in pecans; cook until pecans are coated and sugar turns light brown. Pour praline onto wax paper. Cool; break into coarse pieces. Yield: about ½ cup.

Shortcut Solution: *In a big hurry? You can frost this cake with plain frosting minus the nuts and vanilla, and forgo making the garnishes.*

Using an offset spatula makes frosting cake layers a breeze.

For best results, use an electric knife to slice this cake.

Savannah Christmas
Praline-Spice Cake

CUPS OF CHRISTMAS CHEER

Toast the season with a sip of one of these festive drinks.
They're a spirited group, but we offer serving options sans alcohol, as well.
Serve some hot, some chilled, and all with pleasure.

SPICED CHERRY-APPLE CIDER

Bing cherries, vanilla bean, and peppercorns give this cider fresh appeal. It's equally good served warm or chilled. It's simmered in a slow cooker, so a wonderful aroma fills your home all day.

2   (15-ounce) cans pitted Bing cherries in heavy syrup, undrained
12 cups apple cider
¾   cup firmly packed dark brown sugar
2   tablespoons peeled, grated fresh ginger
15 whole cloves
15 whole black peppercorns
3   (3") cinnamon sticks
1   vanilla bean, split
Cinnamon sticks (optional)

Drain 1 can of cherries. Process drained and undrained cherries in a blender on HIGH until smooth, stopping to scrape down sides.

Combine cherries, cider, sugar, and ginger in a 4½-quart electric slow cooker. Place cloves and next 3 ingredients on an 8" square of cheesecloth; tie with string, and add to slow cooker. Cover and cook on LOW 8 hours. Discard spice bag. Strain cider, discarding pulp. Return cider to slow cooker; serve warm with cinnamon stick stirrers, if desired. Yield: 13 cups.

Plug in the slow cooker. It's a great way to serve hot cider at a party.

TOASTED COCONUT NOG   Make Ahead

Rum, bourbon, and coconut milk lend tropical flair to time-honored eggnog. The recipe doubles easily for a party.

4   egg yolks
2   (13.5-ounce) cans coconut milk
½   cup sugar
1   teaspoon vanilla extract
1   teaspoon almond extract
⅓   cup Malibu rum
⅓   cup bourbon
1   cup whipping cream
Ground nutmeg
Toasted sweetened flaked coconut (optional)

Whisk together first 3 ingredients in a heavy saucepan. Cook over medium heat, stirring often, 5 to 6 minutes or to 160°. Remove from heat, and stir in flavorings. Place plastic wrap directly over surface, and chill at least 4 hours.

Stir in rum and bourbon. Beat whipping cream at medium speed with an electric mixer until soft peaks form; fold into nog. Sprinkle each serving with nutmeg and, if desired, toasted coconut. Yield: about 7 cups.

Nonalcoholic Nog: *Omit the rum and bourbon. It still tastes great and is plenty rich.*

Spiced Cherry-Apple Cider

Toasted Coconut Nog

WINTERY WHITE WINE PUNCH

This cozy punch is spiced for the season with cinnamon, cardamom, and nutmeg.

2   (750-milliliter) bottles semi-dry white wine (we tested with Chenin Blanc)
3   (12-ounce) cans pear nectar
1   (6-ounce) package dried apricots
1   (5-ounce) package dried apples
1   cup golden raisins
¾   cup sugar
1   orange, sliced
2   teaspoons vanilla extract
3   (3") cinnamon sticks
10 cardamom pods
1   whole nutmeg, split

Combine first 8 ingredients in a Dutch oven. Place 3 cinnamon sticks, cardamom, and nutmeg on a 6" square of cheesecloth; tie with string. Add spice bag to wine.

Bring to a simmer over medium heat, stirring occasionally. Cover, remove from heat, and steep 1 hour.

Pour wine through a wire-mesh strainer into a large bowl, discarding spice bag. Serve warm, let cool to room temperature, or chill and serve over ice. Yield: 10 cups.

Note: *Save strained fruit to make Dried Fruit Chutney (page 109).*

Nonalcoholic Punch: *Substitute 6 cups white grape juice for the wine.*

RUBY CHAMPAGNE COCKTAIL

A blend of cranberry juice, orange liqueur, and champagne helps ring in the holidays with sparkle.

2   tablespoons cranberry juice
1   tablespoon orange liqueur
1   teaspoon grenadine
½   cup dry champagne

Place first 3 ingredients in a champagne flute; pour champagne into flute. Yield: 1 cocktail.

Mock Ruby Cocktail: *Combine 1 tablespoon orange juice and 1 tablespoon grenadine in a flute or other festive glass. Add crushed ice to glass, filling three-fourths full. Pour ¼ cup cranberry juice over ice. Finish filling glass with ¼ cup ginger ale. Yield: 1 cocktail.*

BUTTERSCOTCH LATTE

Sip this warming after-dinner drink around the fire on a chilly night.

4   cups boiling water
2   tablespoons instant coffee granules
¾   cup butterscotch schnapps
2   cups milk, warm
2   tablespoons sugar
Canned whipped dessert topping
Cinnamon sugar

Pour boiling water over coffee granules, stirring until coffee granules dissolve. Stir in schnapps; pour into 6 mugs.

Combine warm milk and sugar; pour into a blender, and process at HIGH for about 1 minute. (Milk will become frothy.) Divide milk and froth evenly into mugs. Top each serving with dessert topping, and sprinkle with cinnamon sugar. Serve warm. Yield: 6 cups.

Nonalcoholic Latte: *Substitute ¾ cup butterscotch ice cream topping for butterscotch schnapps.*

Substitution: *If you don't keep instant coffee on hand, you can use 4 cups brewed coffee in this latte. (Omit 4 cups of boiling water.)*

Mock Ruby Cocktails

BITE-SIZE WITH BIG FLAVOR

Plan your next gathering around some of these tasty morsels
meant for a holiday open house.

Spicy Sausage Won Ton Cups

SPICY SAUSAGE WON TON CUPS

Jalapeño pepper and hot pork sausage fire up these crispy
fluted cups.

1   pound hot ground pork sausage

1½ cups (6 ounces) shredded Cheddar cheese

1½ cups (6 ounces) shredded Monterey Jack cheese

½   cup Ranch-style dressing

⅓   cup chopped pimiento-stuffed olives

⅓   cup finely chopped red bell pepper

1   jalapeño pepper, seeded and minced

1   (16-ounce) package won ton wrappers (3½" squares)

Brown sausage in a large skillet over medium-high heat, stirring until it crumbles and is no longer pink; drain on paper towels. Combine sausage and next 6 ingredients.

Coat 4 miniature (1¾") muffin pans with cooking spray. Place won ton wrappers in pans, using fingers to create fluted shape. Lightly spray wrappers with cooking spray. Bake at 350° for 8 minutes, turning pans after 4 minutes.

Spoon 1 heaping tablespoon filling into each won ton cup. Bake at 350° for 9 to 10 minutes or until browned and thoroughly heated. Remove from pans and serve hot. Yield: 3½ dozen.

PARMESAN AND HERB PASTRY PUFFS

Rosemary, thyme, and basil impart herbal delight to these small savory cream puffs. Serve them as is, or see our ideas below right for fillings.

1   cup water
½   cup butter
½   teaspoon salt
¼   teaspoon freshly ground pepper
¼   teaspoon dry mustard
1   cup all-purpose flour
4   large eggs
1   cup plus 2 tablespoons freshly grated Parmesan cheese, divided
1   tablespoon chopped fresh or 1 teaspoon dried basil
1   teaspoon chopped fresh or 1 teaspoon dried rosemary, crushed
½   teaspoon chopped fresh or ¼ teaspoon dried thyme
1   large egg, lightly beaten

Combine first 5 ingredients in a medium saucepan; bring to a boil over high heat. Reduce heat to medium-high; add flour all at once, stirring vigorously until mixture leaves sides of pan and forms a smooth ball. Remove from heat, and cool 1 to 2 minutes.

Add 4 eggs, 1 at a time, beating vigorously with a wooden spoon after each addition; beat until dough is smooth. Stir in 1 cup cheese and herbs.

Drop pastry by rounded tablespoonfuls 1" apart onto lightly greased baking sheets. Brush tops with beaten egg, and sprinkle with remaining 2 tablespoons cheese.

Bake at 400° for 16 to 18 minutes or until golden and puffed. Remove from oven, and let stand on baking sheets for 2 to 3 minutes. Remove and serve hot. Yield: 2½ dozen.

Make Ahead: *Store puffs overnight in an airtight container at room temperature, and reheat on an aluminum foil-lined baking sheet at 350° for 8 minutes or until thoroughly heated. Freeze puffs up to 1 month in an airtight container or zip-top plastic freezer bags, and reheat on an aluminum foil-lined baking sheet at 350° for 10 to 12 minutes or until thoroughly heated. There's no need to thaw them.*

FOR ENTERTAINING

Split puffs and fill with smoked salmon and crème fraîche, assorted soft cheeses, spinach dip (shown below), flavored cream cheese and sun-dried tomatoes, chicken salad (shown below), or little bites of ham, turkey, or beef tenderloin.

Parmesan and Herb Pastry Puffs filled with store-bought spinach dip and chicken salad

CORN AND CRAB FRITTERS WITH SPICY DIPPING SAUCE

Make Ahead

These chunky crab fritters are crisp on the outside and soft on the inside. Make their zippy sauce ahead to save on preparation time.

1   tablespoon butter or margarine
2   tablespoons minced shallot
3   garlic cloves, minced
2   jalapeño peppers, seeded and minced
2   cups frozen whole kernel corn, thawed
2   green onions, thinly sliced
½   cup all-purpose flour
¼   cup semolina flour (see Note)
1   tablespoon sugar
1   teaspoon baking powder
1   teaspoon salt
¼   teaspoon freshly ground black pepper
⅛   teaspoon ground red pepper
2   large eggs, separated
¾   cup buttermilk
½   pound fresh lump crabmeat, drained
Vegetable oil
Salt
Spicy Dipping Sauce

Melt butter in a large skillet over medium-high heat; add shallot, garlic, and jalapeño pepper, and sauté 1 minute. Add corn and green onions, and sauté 2 to 3 minutes. Set aside.

Combine flours and next 5 ingredients in a large bowl. Lightly beat egg yolks; add buttermilk to yolks. Stir sautéed vegetables and buttermilk mixture into flour mixture. Fold in crabmeat.

Beat egg whites at high speed with an electric mixer until soft peaks form. Gently fold half of beaten egg white into crabmeat batter. Fold in remaining beaten egg white.

Pour oil to depth of 2" into a large heavy skillet; heat to 375° over medium-high heat. Shape about 2 tablespoons batter into a fritter by rounding between edges of 2 large spoons. Drop fritters into hot oil, 4 or 5 at a time, and cook 3 minutes or until golden, turning once. Drain on paper towels. Transfer fritters to a baking sheet; sprinkle lightly with salt, and keep warm in a 300° oven. Repeat process with remaining batter. Serve fritters with Spicy Dipping Sauce. Yield: 2 dozen.

Note: *Find semolina flour (coarsely ground durum wheat flour) in your grocer's baking aisle. Its coarse texture lends crispness to the fritters. You can substitute all-purpose flour if you can't find semolina, but the texture will be a little softer.*

SPICY DIPPING SAUCE

1   cup mayonnaise
1   green onion, thinly sliced
1   tablespoon white wine vinegar
2   teaspoons Dijon mustard
½   teaspoon ground red pepper
¼   teaspoon freshly ground black pepper
½   teaspoon hot pepper sauce (we tested with Crystal)

Combine all ingredients in a bowl; cover and chill at least 1 hour. Yield: 1¼ cups.

FOR ENTERTAINING

Serve leftover dipping sauce with crab cakes or boiled shrimp.

Corn and Crab Fritters with Spicy Dipping Sauce

Roasted Olives

ROASTED OLIVES

Marinated olives always seem to go fast at holiday parties. This recipe roasts a gutsy mix of whole olives doused in garlic and rosemary.

3　cups assorted whole olives (we tested with Niçoise, cracked green olives, Picholine, and kalamata)
¼　cup olive oil
4　garlic cloves, thinly sliced
2　tablespoons chopped fresh rosemary
1　tablespoon grated lemon rind
½　teaspoon freshly ground black pepper
½　teaspoon fennel seeds, crushed
¼　teaspoon dried crushed red pepper

Combine all ingredients in a large bowl. Let stand at room temperature at least 15 minutes or up to several hours to allow flavors to blend.

Place olives in a single layer on an aluminum foil-lined pan. Roast at 425° for 10 to 12 minutes, stirring occasionally. Serve warm or let cool to room temperature. Yield: 3 cups.

OLIVE ETIQUETTE

Ever wonder what to do with olive pits when munching on whole olives at a party? Simply drop the olive pit into the palm of your hand and put the pit on your plate.

SMOKED GOUDA- AND APPLE-STUFFED MUSHROOMS

Tangy bits of Granny Smith apple and ground pecans enhance the smoky, meaty flavor of Gouda cheese in these mushrooms stuffed to overflowing with goodness.

2　pounds very large fresh mushrooms (about 30)
2　tablespoons butter or margarine
¼　cup finely chopped onion
1　garlic clove, minced
2　cups (8 ounces) shredded smoked Gouda cheese
¼　cup soft breadcrumbs (homemade)
1　Granny Smith apple, chopped
¼　teaspoon salt
¼　teaspoon freshly ground pepper
3　tablespoons ground pecans
1　tablespoon butter or margarine, melted

Remove and chop mushroom stems; set mushroom caps aside.

Melt 2 tablespoons butter in a large skillet over medium heat. Add mushroom stems, onion, and garlic; sauté 3 to 5 minutes or until tender. Remove from heat. Stir in cheese and next 4 ingredients. Spoon evenly into mushroom caps; place caps on a rack in a broiler pan.

Combine pecans and 1 tablespoon melted butter. Sprinkle evenly over each filled mushroom cap. Bake at 350° for 15 to 17 minutes or until thoroughly heated. Change oven setting to broil, and broil mushrooms 1 to 2 minutes or just until browned on top. Yield: 30 appetizers.

TOMATO AND TWO CHEESE CROSTINI

Swiss cheese and blue cheese comprise the dynamic duo atop crisp Melba crackers. Bits of garlic, dried tomatoes, toasted pecans, and green onion kick up the flavor.

48 plain Melba toast rounds
1 garlic clove, halved
20 dried tomato halves in oil, drained and finely chopped
2 garlic cloves, minced
1 cup (4 ounces) shredded Swiss cheese
1 cup crumbled blue cheese
½ cup chopped pecans, toasted
¼ teaspoon freshly ground pepper
4 green onions, thinly sliced

Place crackers in a single layer on a parchment paper-lined baking sheet. Rub cut sides of halved garlic clove over tops of crackers.

Combine tomatoes and next 5 ingredients in a bowl, stirring until blended. Gently stir in green onions. Let stand 15 minutes for cheese to soften and to allow flavors to blend. Spread 1 heaping teaspoon cheese evenly over each cracker. Bake at 400° for 5 to 7 minutes or until cheese is melted and bubbly. Serve hot. Yield: 4 dozen.

CHOCOLATE-CHERRY BROWNIES   Make Ahead

A splash of bourbon in these decadent bites boosts the bitter-sweet chocolate flavor. Baking them in miniature muffin pans makes them easy to serve.

2 large eggs
¾ cup sugar
⅓ cup vegetable oil
3 (1-ounce) bittersweet chocolate squares, melted
2 teaspoons bourbon
½ teaspoon vanilla extract
⅔ cup all-purpose flour
½ teaspoon baking powder
⅛ teaspoon salt
⅓ cup coarsely chopped pecans, toasted
⅓ cup sweetened dried cherries, chopped
⅓ cup semisweet chocolate mini-morsels
Powdered sugar (optional)

Beat eggs in a large mixing bowl at medium speed with an electric mixer. Gradually add sugar, beating until thick and pale. Add oil and next 3 ingredients, beating until blended.

Combine flour, baking powder, and salt; gradually add to chocolate, beating until blended. Stir in pecans, cherries, and mini-morsels. Spoon batter into greased miniature (1¾") muffin pans, filling three-fourths full. Bake at 350° for 12 minutes. Remove from oven; cool in pans on a wire rack 15 minutes. Remove from pans; cool completely on wire rack. Dust with powdered sugar, if desired. Yield: about 3 dozen.

LEMON-COCONUT BITES

Coconut adds a new complement to the classic lemon bar.

1½ cups all-purpose flour
½ cup powdered sugar
⅛ teaspoon salt
¾ cup butter, cut into pieces
2 large eggs
1 cup sugar
2 tablespoons all-purpose flour
¼ teaspoon baking powder
1 tablespoon grated lemon rind
3 tablespoons fresh lemon juice
¾ teaspoon vanilla extract
¼ teaspoon coconut extract
1 (3.5-ounce) can sweetened flaked coconut, coarsely chopped
3 tablespoons butter, cut into pieces
2 tablespoons all-purpose flour
Powdered sugar

Lightly grease an 8" square pan; line with heavy-duty aluminum foil, allowing several inches of foil to extend over ends of pan. Grease foil.

Combine 1½ cups flour, ½ cup powdered sugar, and salt in a bowl. Add ¾ cup butter and combine with a pastry blender until crumbly. Press mixture into bottom of pan. Bake at 325° for 25 to 28 minutes or until crust is lightly browned. Cool 15 minutes.

Whisk together eggs, 1 cup sugar, 2 tablespoons flour, and next 5 ingredients in a medium bowl. Pour lemon filling over crust.

Combine coconut, 3 tablespoons butter, and 2 table-spoons flour with a pastry blender until crumbly. Sprinkle evenly over filling. Bake at 325° for 35 minutes or until set. Cool completely in pan on a wire rack. Lift uncut brownies from pan, using aluminum foil handles. Cut into squares or triangles, or cut out circles, using a 1½" round cutter. Dust with powdered sugar. Yield: 16 squares or circles, or 32 triangles.

FOR ENTERTAINING

If you cut out these little cookies into festive rounds, you'll have some delicious lemony scraps leftover. We recommend stirring these sweet nibbles into vanilla ice cream and serving it as a gourmet dessert.

Lemon-Coconut Bites

ALMOST ONE-DISH DINNERS

*These entrées are packed with meat and vegetables, leaving little else to do to get dinner on the table. Our **Add on** serving suggestions take the guesswork out of the go-withs.*

Scalloped Potato Duo with Ham

CHICKEN AND BISCUITS

Have an abundance of leftover turkey from your holiday meal? Feel free to substitute turkey for the chicken in this homestyle recipe.

1   whole chicken, cut up, if desired
1   teaspoon salt
3   carrots, chopped
3   celery ribs, chopped
3   large leeks (white and light green color only), chopped
1   medium onion, halved and sliced
1   teaspoon olive oil
1   cup dry white wine
1   teaspoon salt
1   cup frozen sweet peas
2   cups all-purpose flour
1   tablespoon baking powder
½   teaspoon salt
1   tablespoon chopped fresh rosemary
5   tablespoons cold butter or margarine, cut into pieces
¾   cup (3 ounces) shredded sharp Cheddar cheese
1   large egg
½   cup half-and-half
1   tablespoon butter or margarine, melted

Place chicken in a Dutch oven; add 1 teaspoon salt and water to cover. Bring to a boil; reduce heat, cover and simmer 1 hour. Drain chicken, reserving 4 cups broth. Debone chicken.

Sauté carrot, celery, leek, and onion in oil in Dutch oven over medium-high heat 5 minutes. Add chicken to Dutch oven; add reserved broth, wine, and 1 teaspoon salt. Bring to a boil; simmer, uncovered, over medium-high heat 20 minutes. Remove from heat, and stir in peas.

Combine flour, baking powder, ½ teaspoon salt, and rosemary. Cut in butter with a pastry blender until crumbly. Add cheese. Combine egg and half-and-half. Add to dry ingredients, stirring with a fork until a dough is formed.

Drop biscuit dough over top of chicken and vegetables, forming 8 biscuits. Brush with melted butter. Bake, uncovered, at 425° for 20 minutes or until top is bubbly and biscuits are done. Yield: 6 to 8 servings.

Make Ahead: *Boil chicken according to recipe; reserve broth and debone chicken. Keep in refrigerator overnight. Prepare biscuit dough; shape into 8 biscuits and chill overnight. Finish preparing chicken recipe base the next day; top with biscuits and bake.*

SCALLOPED POTATO DUO WITH HAM

Two types of potato, nutty Gruyère cheese, and salty ham give this entrée unusual appeal.

1   medium onion, coarsely chopped
1   tablespoon vegetable oil
3   garlic cloves, finely chopped
2   sweet potatoes, peeled and cut into ¼" slices (about 1½ pounds)
2   baking potatoes, peeled and cut into ¼" slices (about 1½ pounds)
½   cup all-purpose flour
1   teaspoon salt
¼   teaspoon pepper
2   cups chopped ham
2   cups (8 ounces) shredded Gruyère cheese, divided
1¾ cups whipping cream
2   tablespoons butter, cut into pieces

Sauté onion in oil over medium-high heat 5 minutes. Add garlic; cook 30 seconds. Remove from heat and set aside. Place potatoes in a large bowl.

Combine flour, salt, and pepper; sprinkle over potatoes, tossing to coat. Arrange half of potato mixture in a greased 13" x 9" baking dish or 3-quart gratin dish. Top with onion, ham, and 1 cup cheese. Top with remaining potato mixture. Pour cream over potato mixture. Dot with butter, and cover with aluminum foil.

Bake at 400° for 50 minutes. Uncover, top with remaining 1 cup cheese, and bake 20 more minutes or until potatoes are tender and cheese is browned. Let stand 10 minutes before serving. Yield: 6 to 8 servings.

Chicken and Sausage Cassoulet

CHICKEN AND SAUSAGE CASSOULET

Make Ahead

Add ons

• crusty bread
• sautéed cabbage

Bring a big appetite to the table to greet this hearty French casserole of sausage, chicken, and great Northern beans. It starts on the stove and finishes in the oven, giving you time to do other things.

1   pound dried great Northern beans
1   tablespoon vegetable oil
3   chicken leg quarters
3   large carrots, cut into 1" pieces
3   celery ribs, chopped
2   onions, chopped
1   (14.5-ounce) can diced tomatoes, undrained
½   cup dry white wine
3¾ cups chicken broth
2   fresh thyme sprigs
1   bay leaf
1   pound kielbasa, cut into 6 pieces
1   teaspoon salt
½   teaspoon pepper

Sort and wash beans. Place beans in a Dutch oven; add water 2" above beans. Bring to a boil; boil 2 minutes. Cover, remove from heat, and let stand 1 hour. Drain.

Heat oil in an oven-proof Dutch oven over medium-high heat until hot. Add chicken, and cook 3 to 4 minutes on each side or until browned. Remove chicken, reserving drippings in pan; set aside. Sauté carrot, celery, and onion in drippings 8 minutes. Stir in tomatoes and wine. Bring to a boil; reduce heat, and simmer, uncovered, 2 minutes. Stir in beans, chicken broth, thyme, and bay leaf. Place chicken, skin side up, on top of beans. Bring cassoulet to a boil.

Bake, uncovered, at 375° for 1 hour. Stir in kielbasa, salt, and pepper; rearrange chicken, skin side up, on top. Bake, uncovered, 25 more minutes or until most of the liquid is absorbed and beans are tender. Let stand 10 minutes before serving. Yield: 6 servings.

Make Ahead: *If you plan to serve cassoulet the next day, prepare recipe in full, let cool, and debone chicken before chilling. Reheat, covered, over medium-low heat, stirring often.*

HEARTY CLAM CHOWDER

Add ons
• green salad
• oyster crackers

Warm up with a bowlful of this rich chowder loaded with clams and brimming with chunks of potato.

4   bacon slices, chopped
3   celery ribs, chopped
2   carrots, chopped
1   onion, chopped
2   large russet potatoes, peeled and cubed
4   (6½-ounce) cans minced clams, undrained
2   (8-ounce) bottles clam juice
1½ cups water
1   sprig fresh thyme
1   teaspoon salt
¼   teaspoon pepper
1½ cups milk
⅓   cup all-purpose flour
Garnish: fresh thyme

Cook bacon in a Dutch oven over medium-high heat 4 minutes or until almost crisp. Add celery, carrot, and onion; cook 5 minutes, stirring often.

Stir in potato and next 6 ingredients. Bring to a boil; reduce heat, and simmer, uncovered, 20 minutes. Whisk together milk and flour until smooth. Stir into chowder; simmer 10 minutes or until thickened, stirring often. Remove thyme sprig before serving. If desired, serve chowder in sourdough bread bowls. Garnish, if desired. Yield: 10½ cups.

Edible Bread Bowls: *Buy small round loaves of sourdough or other bakery bread. Cut off top of each loaf and scoop out center, leaving a thick shell, about ¾". Toast bread bowls, if desired. Fill each bowl with chowder. (Omit serving oyster crackers if serving chowder in bread bowls.) Use the scooped-out bread to make croutons.*

Hearty Clam Chowder

Béchamel Lasagna with
Butternut Squash and Sausage

BÉCHAMEL LASAGNA WITH BUTTERNUT SQUASH AND SAUSAGE

Lasagna dresses fancy for the holidays with spicy pork sausage teamed with tender butternut squash and a silky white sauce.

1   pound hot ground pork sausage
3   pounds butternut squash
1   onion, coarsely chopped
2   tablespoons olive oil
1¼ teaspoons salt, divided
12 uncooked lasagna noodles
5   tablespoons butter or margarine
2   garlic cloves, thinly sliced
½   cup all-purpose flour
5   cups milk
1   cup finely shredded Parmesan cheese
½   teaspoon ground nutmeg
3   cups (12 ounces) shredded mozzarella cheese

Brown sausage in a large skillet over medium-high heat, stirring until it crumbles and is no longer pink; drain and set aside. Wipe drippings from skillet with a paper towel. Set aside.

Peel squash; cut in half lengthwise. Remove seeds, and slice squash into ¼" slices. Place squash in a roasting pan. Add onion, oil, and ¼ teaspoon salt; toss well. Bake, uncovered, at 425° for 25 to 30 minutes or just until squash is tender, stirring twice. Remove from oven, and set aside.

Cook lasagna noodles according to package directions; drain. Set aside. Melt butter in a large skillet over medium-high heat. Add garlic, and cook 30 seconds. Whisk in flour until smooth. Cook over low heat, 1 minute, whisking constantly. Gradually whisk in milk. Cook over medium heat, whisking constantly, 3 to 4 minutes or until thickened and bubbly. Stir in Parmesan cheese, remaining 1 teaspoon salt, and nutmeg.

Spread 1 cup béchamel sauce in bottom of a greased 13" x 9" baking dish. Layer with 4 noodles, half of sausage, and half of squash. Top with ¾ cup sauce, 1 cup mozzarella cheese, and 4 noodles. Repeat layers with remaining ingredients, ending with sauce and mozzarella cheese.

Cover and bake at 375° for 20 minutes. Uncover and bake 30 more minutes. Let stand 10 minutes before serving. Yield: 8 to 10 servings.

Make Ahead: *Making lasagna can be a big task. Try these steps the day before to get ahead: Brown sausage; refrigerate overnight. Roast the squash and onion and refrigerate overnight. Then finish preparing and baking lasagna the next day. Or you can prepare lasagna in full and refrigerate overnight, unbaked. Then bake the next day.*

SHORT RIBS BRAISED IN WINE

Red wine and beef broth make a rich braising liquid for these fall-off-the-bone tender ribs.

3½ to 4 pounds short ribs, trimmed (8 to 9 ribs)
1   teaspoon salt
1   teaspoon pepper
1   tablespoon vegetable oil
1   onion, chopped
5   garlic cloves, minced
2   tablespoons tomato paste
2   cups red wine
1   bay leaf
1   sprig fresh thyme
1   (14-ounce) can beef broth
4   large carrots, cut into 2" pieces
2   turnips, cut into 2" pieces

Sprinkle ribs with salt and pepper. Heat oil in a large Dutch oven over medium-high heat until hot. Add half of ribs. Cook 10 minutes or until browned, turning once or twice. Remove ribs to a plate. Repeat procedure with remaining ribs.

Add onion and garlic to pan; sauté 3 minutes. Stir in tomato paste; cook 2 minutes. Add wine, bay leaf, and thyme. Bring to a boil. Return ribs to pan; add broth. Cover, reduce heat, and simmer 2 hours. Add carrot and turnip pieces. Bring to a boil. Cover, reduce heat, and simmer 1 hour and 15 minutes or until meat and vegetables are very tender. Discard bay leaf and thyme sprig before serving. Yield: 4 to 5 servings.

WHERE TO FIND IT

Source information is current at the time of publication, but we cannot guarantee availability of items. If an item is not listed, its source is unknown.

page 11—angel: Christine's; 2822 Petticoat Lane; Mountain Brook, AL 35223; (205) 871-8297

pages 11 and 15—wreaths, garland: Martin & Son Wholesale Florist; 2901 3rd Avenue South; Birmingham, AL 35223; (205) 251-7673

pages 20 and 21—pillow: Seasons of Cannon Falls™; www.seasonsofcannonfalls.com for a retailer near you

red mirror: Harmony Landing; 2925 18th Street South; Birmingham, AL 35209; (205) 871-0585; harmonylanding@aol.com

snowflake ornaments: Christmas & Co.; P.O. Box 130037; Birmingham, AL 35213; (205) 943-0020; www.christmasandco.com

page 23—berry cone: Lamb's Ears Ltd.; 3138 Cahaba Heights Road; Birmingham, AL 35243; (205) 969-3138

page 24—red ornaments, berry candle wreath: TAG (Trade Associates Group); (773) 871-1300

Sabre flatware: Table d'Art; 250 Greenwich Avenue; Greenwich, CT 06830; (203) 869-8082; motioneast@aol.com

berry garland: Smith & Hawken; (800) 981-9888; www.smithandhawken.com

bowls, plate ornaments, flatware ornaments: Seasons of Cannon Falls™; www.seasonsofcannonfalls.com for a retailer near you

page 25—moss-wrapped ribbon: Christmas & Co.; P.O. Box 130037; Birmingham, AL 35213; (205) 943-0020; www.christmasandco.com

page 30—table, chairs: Summer Classics; P.O. Box 1300; Columbiana, AL 35051; (888) 868-4267; www.summerclassics.com

dishes: Vietri; 343 Elizabeth Brady Road; Hillsborough, NC 27278; (800) 277-5933; www.vietri.com

napkins: TAG (Trade Associates Group); (773) 871-1300

copper cache pots: Smith & Hawken; (800) 981-9888; www.smithandhawken.com

flatware: Alain Saint Joanis; (602) 944-2898; www.alain-saint-joanis.com

page 38—Merry Christmas blocks: Flora; 1911 Oxmoor Road; Homewood, AL 35209; (205) 871-4004

postcard dish towels: Taylor & Coultas, Inc.; 220 East State Street; Jacksonville, IL 62650; (217) 245-9188; www.taylorandcoultas.com

page 39—santa, tree candleholder: Attic Antiques; 5620 Cahaba Valley Road;

Birmingham, AL 35242; (205) 991-6887

page 40—garland: Martin & Son Wholesale Florist; 2901 3rd Avenue South; Birmingham, AL 35223; (205) 251-7673

bowl: Cast Art; 1713 2nd Avenue South; Birmingham, AL 35233; (205) 324-3936

crystal candleholder: Tricia's Treasures; 2700 19th Place South; Homewood, AL 35209; (205) 871-9779

tall angel with halo, small angels: Christmas & Co.; P.O. Box 130037; Birmingham, AL 35213; (205) 943-0020; www.christmasandco.com

page 41—pewter pieces, cones, reindeer, boot: Attic Antiques; 5620 Cahaba Valley Road; Birmingham, AL 35242; (205) 991-6887

church, Santa, pewter-colored ornaments: Christmas & Co.; P.O. Box 130037; Birmingham, AL 35213; (205) 943-0020; www.christmasandco.com

candy: Hammond's Candies; (888) CANDY99; www.hammondscandies.com

pages 42 and 43—gold angels: Flora; 1911 Oxmoor Road; Homewood, AL 35209; (205) 871-4004

gold ornaments: TAG (Trade Associates Group); (773) 871-1300

page 44—candy: Hammond's Candies; (888) CANDY99; www.hammondscandies.com

page 45—antique transferware: Henhouse Antiques; 1900 Cahaba Road; Birmingham, AL 35223; (205) 918-0505

square pedestals: Abbey Lane; 784 Brookwood Village; Birmingham, AL 35209 (205) 879-7122

page 50—Timber® candles (cranberry): Vance Kitira; (800) 646-6360 for a retailer near you

pages 52–55—ribbon, bead garland: Christmas & Co.; P.O. Box 130037; Birmingham, AL 35213; (205) 943-0020; www.christmasandco.com

page 56—ball ornaments: Mariposa; (800) 788-1304; www.mariposa-gift.com for a retailer near you

small gold ornaments: TAG (Trade Associates Group); (773) 871-1300

page 57—topiary, container: Leaf 'N Petal; 2817 Cahaba Road; Birmingham, AL 35223; (205) 871-3832

pages 57 and 167—red dishes: Pier 1 Imports; (800) 245-4595; www.pier1.com

pages 58, 62, 64, and 65—silver nut bowl: Mariposa; (800) 788-1304; www.mariposa-gift.com for a retailer near you

pewter tray: MATCH; Eight Hope Street; Jersey City, NJ 07307; (201) 792-9444; www.match1995.com

pages 60, 61, and 66—white dinnerware, red napkins: Williams-Sonoma; (800) 541-2233; www.williams-sonoma.com

flowers, wreaths: Martin & Son Wholesale Florist; 2901 3rd Avenue South; Birmingham, AL 35223; (205) 251-7673

silver cherubs, serving bowl, silver wine caddy: Tricia's Treasures; 2700 19th Place South; Homewood, AL 35209; (205) 871-9779

glasses: Bromberg & Co.; (800) 633-4616; www.brombergs.com

page 70—trumpet angel: Flora; 1911 Oxmoor Road; Homewood, AL 35209; (205) 871-4004

dessert plates, mugs (Holly Ribbons pattern): Bromberg & Co.; (800) 633-4616; www.brombergs.com

pages 72 and 73—plates: Mariposa; (800) 788-1304; www.mariposa-gift.com for a retailer near you

red serving bowl: Crate & Barrel; (800) 996-9960; www.crateandbarrel.com

vases: Pottery Barn; (888) 779-5176; www.potterybarn.com

red pitcher: Bauer Pottery Company; (888) 213-0800; www.bauerla.com

page 81—cake stand: Christine's; 2822 Petticoat Lane; Mountain Brook, AL 35223; (205) 871-8297

Barbara Eigen striped dishes: Tesori; 618 Valley Road; Upper Montclair, NJ 07044; (973) 655-1511; www.tesori.com

platter: Present Tense; (800) 282-7117; www.presenttense.com for a retailer near you

page 88—plates, teacups, and kettle: Bauer Pottery Company; (888) 213-0800; www.bauerla.com

frosted tumblers: CASA Collection; (415) 346-5008 for a retailer near you

page 89—reindeer centerpiece: King's House Antiques; 2418 Montevallo Road; Mountain Brook, AL 35223; (205) 871-5787

dinnerware (Holiday Collection): Louisville Stoneware; 731 Brent Street; Louisville, KY 40204; (800) 626-1800; www.louisvillestoneware.com

glasses: Mariposa; (800) 788-1304; www.mariposa-gift.com for a retailer near you page 92 and 101—striped wrapping paper: Midori, Inc.; 708 Sixth Avenue North; Seattle, WA 98109; (800) 659-3049; www.midoriribbon.com

pages 93 and 106—Cote Table dishes: Kiss That Frog; 2310 Fourth Street; Berkeley, CA 94710; (510) 524-7611

pillows: Taylor & Coultas, Inc.; 220 East State Street; Jacksonville, IL 62650; (217) 245-9188; www.taylorandcoultas.com

page 94—red basket: TAG (Trade Associates Group); (773) 871-1300

felt ribbon (green and brown): Mokuba New York/Jkarta; 55 West 39th Street; New York, NY 10018; (212) 869-8900

page 95—brown crinkle ribbon: Just Accents, Inc.; (888) 389-0550; www.justaccentsny.com

green ribbon: Mokuba New York/Jkarta; 55 West 39th Street; New York, NY 10018; (212) 869-8900

vintage postcards: Crestwood Antiques; 5514 Crestwood Boulevard; Birmingham, AL 35210; (205) 595-0095; www.crestwoodantiques.com

page 96—candy: Hammond's Candies; (888) CANDY99; www.hammondscandies.com

ribbon: Michaels Arts and Crafts; (800) 642-4235; www.michaels.com

page 99—snowman mugs and plates: TAG (Trade Associates Group); (773) 871-1300

trees, snowmen: Christmas & Co.; P.O. Box 130037; Birmingham, AL 35213; (205) 943-0020; www.christmasandco.com

page 101—holly leaf ornament: Christmas & Co.; P.O. Box 130037; Birmingham, AL 35213; (205) 943-0020; www.christmasandco.com

page 104—red ornaments: TAG (Trade Associates Group); (773) 871-1300

page 111—wooden baking molds: Crate & Barrel; (800) 996-9960; www.crateandbarrel.com

page 113—Weck jars: Organized Living; www.organizedliving.com

spreaders: Harmony Landing; 2925 18th Street South; Birmingham, AL 35209; (205) 871-0585; harmonylanding@aol.com

pages 114 and 115—food chopper: Williams-Sonoma; (800) 541-2233; www.williams-sonoma.com

pages 114 and 116—stainless steel scoop: Kitchen Realm; www.kitchenrealm.com

pages 114 and 117—individual quiche pans: Williams-Sonoma; (800) 541-2233; www.williams-sonoma.com

pages 114 and 118—Silpat® baking mat: Sur La Table; (800) 243-0852; www.surlatable.com

pages 114 and 119—pie weights: Williams-Sonoma; (800) 541-2233; www.williams-sonoma.com

French tart pan: Sur La Table; (800) 243-0852; www.surlatable.com

pages 114 and 120—Microplane® grater: Sur La Table; (800) 243-0852; www.surlatable.com

pages 114 and 121—muffin top pan: Baker's Catalogue; (800) 827-6836; www.bakerscatalogue.com

pages 114 and 122—mini springform pans: Williams-Sonoma; (800) 541-2233; www.williams-sonoma.com

pages 114 and 123—farmyard pancake molds: Williams-Sonoma; (800) 541-2233; www.williams-sonoma.com

pages 124 and 129—tray (Christmas tree pattern): Spode; 1265 Glen Avenue; Moorestown, NJ 08057; (856) 866-2900

page 125 and cover—pedestal (Foglia pattern): Vietri; 343 Elizabeth Brady Road; Hillsborough, NC 27278; (800) 277-5933; www.vietri.com

wrapped packages: Midori Inc.; 708 Sixth Avenue North; Seattle, Washington 98109; (800) 659-3049; www.midoriribbon.com

Hermes china (Le jardin de Pythagare pattern): Bromberg & Co.; (800) 633-4616; www.brombergs.com

page 128—Barbara Eigen platter: Tesori; 618 Valley Road; Upper Montclair, NJ 07044; (973) 655-1511; www.tesori.com

mugs (holly sprig pattern): Bridgewater Pottery Ltd.; +44 (0) 20 7371 5489; www.bridgewaterpottery.co.uk

page 130—plate: TAG (Trade Associates Group); (773) 871-1300

plaid bowl: Present Tense; (800) 282-7117; www.presenttense.com for a retailer near you

page 131—soufflé dish: Williams-Sonoma; (800) 541-2233; www.williams-sonoma.com

polka dot bowl: Vietri; 343 Elizabeth Brady Road; Hillsborough, NC 27278; (800) 277-5933; www.vietri.com

page 132—dessert plate: Bromberg & Co.; (800) 633-4616; www.brombergs.com

page 133—dishes: Mariposa; (800) 788-1304; www.mariposa-gift.com for a retailer near you

Sabre flatware: Table d'Art; 250 Greenwich Avenue; Greenwich, CT 06830; (203) 869-8082; motioneast@aol.com

page 134—pie plate: Southern Living At HOME™; www.southernlivingathome.com

Raynaud dishes: Bromberg & Co.; (800) 633-4616; www.brombergs.com

page 137—dinner plate: Mariposa; (800) 788-1304; www.mariposa-gift.com for a retailer near you

page 138—bowl: Anthropologie; (800) 309-2500; www.anthropologie.com

page 139—plate (Palm Frawn pattern): Louisville Stoneware; 731 Brent Street;

Louisville, KY 40204; (800) 626-1800; www.louisvillestoneware.com

page 140—Barbara Eigen platter: Tesori; 618 Valley Road; Upper Montclair, NJ 07044; (973) 655-1511; www.tesori.com

page 142—trifle bowl: Simon Pearce; 120 Wooster Street; New York, NY 10012; (212) 334-2393; www.simonpearce.com

striped bag: TAG (Trade Associates Group), (773) 871-1300

page 144—bowl, mug: Vietri; 343 Elizabeth Brady Road; Hillsborough, NC 27278; (800) 277-5933; www.vietri.com

page 145—platter: Southern Living At HOME™; www.southernlivingathome.com for ordering information

page 148—pedestal, plate (Evergreen pattern): Vietri; 343 Elizabeth Brady Road; Hillsborough, NC 27278; (800) 277-5933; www.vietri.com

napkin: TAG (Trade Associates Group); (773) 871-1300

page 150—Barbara Eigen pedestal: Tesori; 618 Valley Road; Upper Montclair, NJ 07044; (973) 655-1511; www.tesori.com

snowman: Louisville Stoneware; 731 Brent Street; Louisville, KY 40204; (800) 626-1800; www.louisvillestoneware.com

page 153—Cote Table plates and mugs: Kiss That Frog; 2310 Fourth Street; Berkeley, CA 94710; (510) 524-7611

pedestal: Flora; 1911 Oxmoor Road; Homewood, AL 35209; (205) 871-4004

page 157—glasses (Angelica pattern): Amalfi; 745 85th Avenue, Unit L; Oakland, CA 94621; (877) 503-4321; www.amalficollection.com

page 159—green tray: Southern Living At HOME™; www.southernlivingathome.com for ordering information

napkin, tree candleholders: TAG (Trade Associates Group); (773) 871-1300

page 161—Barbara Eigen olive dishes: Tesori; 618 Valley Road; Upper Montclair, NJ 07044; (973) 655-1511; www.tesori.com

page 163—mugs (Christmas Whimsey pattern), plate (Creation Red pattern): Gail Pittman; www.gailpittman.com for a retailer near you

page 164—white casserole: Williams-Sonoma; (800) 541-2233; www.williams-sonoma.com

page 166—bowls: Kiss That Frog; 2310 Fourth Street; Berkeley, CA 94710; (510) 524-7611

mini casserole: Mamma Ro; 211 South 4th Street; Highlands, NC 28741; (828) 526-1924; www.mammaro.com

page 168—casserole: Mariposa; (800) 788-1304; www.mariposa-gift.com for a retailer near you

PATTERNS & INSTRUCTIONS

TAGS IN A TWINKLING *(page 98)*

Enlarge or reduce pattern on
photocopier to desired size.

FESTIVE FRUIT *(pages 54–55)*

To create ribbon-adorned fruit to hang
from a window as shown on pages
54–55, bend a long florist wire in half
and insert both ends of the wire in the
bottom of the fruit. Florist wire is available at crafts and discount stores.

To attach the ribbon hanger, center a
long piece of ribbon across the top of
the fruit, and twist the wire ends to hold
the ribbon in place. Trim the wire. Using
a shorter piece of ribbon, tie a bow around
the ribbon hanger at the top of the fruit.
Use small nails or thumbtacks to secure
the ribbon to the top of the window.

GENERAL INDEX

RECIPE INDEX

Contributors

Editorial Contributors

Rebecca Boggan
Maryanna Brooke
Lorrie Corvin
Adrienne Short Davis
Catherine Fowler
Alicia Frazier
Susan Huff
Alisa Jane Hyde
Janet Jackson
Laurie Knowles
Tim Smith

Thanks to the Following Homeowners

Katherine and Garry Ard
Lauren and Joel Brooks
Julia Ann and Joe Cleage
Judy and Bert Hill
Susan and Don Huff
Allison and Glenn Peters
Lori and Peter Reich
Suzanne and Rocky Stewart
Linda and Jeffrey Stone
Sally and Jeff Threlkeld

Thanks to the Following Birmingham Businesses and Organizations

Altar Blooms
Attic Antiques
Birmingham Antique Mall
The Briarcliff Shop
Briarwood Presbyterian Church
Bridges Antiques
Bromberg & Company
Cast Art
Christine's
Christmas & Co.
Davis Wholesale Florist
Flora
Harmony Landing
Henhouse Antiques
King's Garden
Lamb's Ears Ltd.
Leaf 'N Petal
Martin & Sons Wholesale Florist
Tricia's Treasures

Special Thanks

Seasons of Cannon Falls™,
Cannon Falls, Minnesota

HOLIDAY PLANNING GUIDE

Make your holidays easy and enjoyable with the help of this handy guide. The calendars have plenty of space to note parties and events, and the planning pages provide ample room to write your thoughts on menus, gifts, and entertaining for the holidays. Scattered throughout are dozens of useful tips to make this the most organized, the most carefree Christmas ever!

NOVEMBER

Sunday	Monday	Tuesday	Wednesday
2	3	4	5
9	10	11	12
16	17	18	19
23			
30	24	25	26

2003

Write every special event for the month on this calendar so you won't miss a single thing!

Thursday	Friday	Saturday
		1
6	7	8
13	14	15
20	21	22
Thanksgiving 27	28	29

THINGS TO DO:

DECEMBER

Sunday	Monday	Tuesday	Wednesday
	1	2	3
7	8	9	10
14	15	16	17
21	22	23	Christmas Eve 24
28	29	30	New Year's Eve 31

2003

Thursday	Friday	Saturday
4	5	6
11	12	13
18	19	20
Christmas 25	26	27

THINGS TO DO:

HOLIDAY PARTY COUNTDOWN

A good party plan makes everything go more smoothly on the big day. Our countdown helps you begin your preparations up to six weeks ahead of your event.

4 TO 6 WEEKS AHEAD
- Set the date and time.
- Make your guest list.
- Decide what you'll serve. Consult make-ahead recipe notes. On your calendar, write when you'll prepare or assemble each dish. Order any food you decide to have catered.
- Select invitations if you plan to send them for your party.

3 WEEKS AHEAD
- Mail party invitations. For informal events, send invitations two weeks in advance.

1 TO 2 WEEKS AHEAD
- Check your supply of chairs, serving dishes, flatware, and glassware.
- Make a grocery list. Shop for nonperishables.
- Give some thought to your home's exterior. Plant seasonal flowers in a planter on the front porch, hang a festive wreath, wash front-facing windows—anything to give your place a lift.

2 TO 3 DAYS AHEAD
- Get out china, serving dishes, and utensils. Polish silver.
- Shop for perishables.
- Clean house. If you're too busy, consider hiring a cleaning crew.
- Make place cards.

1 DAY AHEAD
- Plan a centerpiece. Buy flowers or clip greenery and berries from your backyard.
- Prepare dishes that can be made ahead.
- Chill beverages. Make extra ice.
- Anticipate "guest geography." Arrange furniture to maximize seating, pulling service chairs from other rooms. Place occasional or folding tables nearby.

DAY OF THE EVENT
- Set the table. Arrange the centerpiece.
- Finish preparing food, and arrange it on serving dishes. For a buffet or large party, fill additional trays so that you can replenish the table by exchanging a full tray for an empty one.
- Reserve some time for rest. If you're refreshed and relaxed, you'll be able to enjoy your party every bit as much as your guests will.

Menus

*Here are a variety of menu ideas based upon
recipes in the book. We suggest a beverage, appetizer, or dessert
when it really makes the menu great.*

Lasagna Night
FOR 8 TO 10

Béchamel Lasagna with Butternut Squash
and Sausage (p.169)
Broccoli with Pancetta and Lemon (p.69)
Garlic bread
White wine

Comfort Food Supper
FOR 4 TO 5

Short Ribs Braised in Wine (p.169)
Mashed potatoes
Green beans
Red wine
Cream Cheese Pound Cake (p.128)

Holiday Brunch
FOR 12

Turkey Hash x3 (p.144)
Grits
Bacon, Leek, and Gruyère Quiche x2 (p.135)
Fresh fruit
Streusel-Sour Cream Coffee Cake (p.149)
Orange Scones with Dates (p.120)
Spiced Cherry-Apple Cider (p.154)

Wrappin' Up the Weekend
FOR 4

Smoked Turkey Wraps (p.146)
Apple slices
Red and green grapes
Cherry and White Chocolate Oatmeal Cookies (p.116)

Pizza Party
FOR 4 OR 8

Roasted Olives (p.161)
Marinated Mushrooms with Honey and Sage (p.67)
Iron Skillet Pizza Pie (p.134) and/or Chicken Pizza
with Arugula (p.136)
Silky Fudge Sauce (p.109) over ice cream

Christmas Open House
FOR 20

Cranberry Brie (p.65)
Smoky Nuts (p.64)
Turkey-Artichoke Tartlets (p.145)
Spicy Sausage Won Ton Cups (p.158)
Triple Chocolate Clusters (p.129)
Pecan Sticks (p.127)
Toasted Coconut Nog x2 (p.154)
Spiced Cherry-Apple Cider (p.154)

Company Casserole
FOR 6 TO 8

Turkey Tetrazzini (p.144)
Spinach-Pecan Salad x2 (p.130)
Rolls
Butter Coconut Pie (p.127)

Elegant Dinner Party
FOR 8

Smoky Nuts (p.64)
Spinach- and Herb-Stuffed Turkey Roll (p.141)
Gingersnap Sweet Potatoes (p.80)
Swiss-Squash Casserole (p.79)
Rolls
Holiday Lane Cake (p.151)

Cozy Winter Fare
FOR 6

Maple- and Pecan-Glazed Pork Tenderloin (p.137)
Green Peas and Baby Limas with Pine Nuts (p.79)
Carrot Soufflé (p.131)
Cinnamon Mocha Pie (p.132)

Late Night Dessert Fest
FOR 12

Triple Chocolate Clusters (p.129)
Cappuccino Pound Cake (p.128)
Chocolate-Cherry Brownies (p.162)
Butterscotch Latte x2 (p.156)

ENTERTAINING PLANNER

Putting your plans on paper is half the task. Use these pages to write all the important details that will make your holiday entertaining the best it's ever been.

GUEST LIST

Use these lines to list names and phone numbers of guests
you plan to invite to your holiday festivities.

MENU IDEAS

On these lines, jot down page numbers and names of recipes you'd like to add to your menu plans.

PANTRY LIST

List an inventory of what you have and what you
need on these lines.

....

....

....

....

....

....

....

....

....

....

....

....

....

....

....

PARTY TO-DO LIST

Find great entertaining tips in our
10 Party Pointers on page 69.

....

....

....

....

....

....

....

....

....

LAST-MINUTE DETAILS

Use this space to help jog your memory as
party-time approaches.

....

....

....

....

....

....

....

Easy Etiquette

Here are a few things to keep in mind when you're
hosting an event.

- For formal service, present a served dinner plate from
the left of each guest; remove plates from the right.

- For family-style service, pass bowls and platters of
food around the table to the right.

- Serve and remove beverages from the right with the
right hand. Be careful not to collide with other beverage glasses.

- Pick up a guest's glass at the stem or the base,
never near or over the top.

- Keep a napkin in your left hand to wipe drips from
coffee pots or water pitchers.

- As the hostess, take your first bite as soon as you're
seated. Guests will take their cue to begin eating from
you. Once you pick up a piece of flatware, never place
it back on the table; rest it on your plate. Leave the
knife at the upper plate edge with its blade toward the
plate. Leave the fork centered on the plate.

- Remove salt, pepper, butter, and excess flatware
from the table after the main course is cleared away.

CHRISTMAS DINNER PLANNER

Start a new tradition with our Ultimate Southern Christmas Dinner on page 73.
This buffet menu serves 10 to 12 people.

GUEST LIST

On these lines, write the names and phone numbers of guests
you plan to invite to your holiday dinner.

MENU

Check out the Christmas Countdown on page 74
to make planning the holiday feast a breeze.

DINNER TO-DO LIST

Make a list and check it twice, and you're on your way to a carefree meal.

....

....

....

....

....

....

....

....

....

....

....

....

....

....

....

....

....

....

....

....

SETTING UP THE BUFFET

A buffet is the most popular style of meal service, especially for large groups. Set the buffet on a dining room table or other surface, such as a chest, kitchen counter, or sideboard, that will accommodate a stack of dinner plates and serving dishes of food. Since your guests will serve themselves, arrange the buffet using these tips:

• Place serving dishes in an arrangement that allows for easy circulation and traffic flow.

• Set the buffet near the kitchen so that it's easy to refill serving dishes.

• Arrange dishes in logical order. For example, if a dish is to be served over rice, locate the rice first in line.

• Place dressings and sauces close to the dish they complement.

• Serve desserts at one end of the buffet, or place them on a serving cart.

• Arrange beverages on a side table, or serve them from a tray after guests are seated.

Getting Ready

Plan ahead as much as possible for the big Christmas meal, and focus on enjoying friends and family.

• Start the day with an empty dishwasher, and you'll find the task of cleanup more manageable.

• Designate an area for coffee, tea, juices, water, and any other beverages. Your family and friends can serve themselves and create an immediate opportunity to feel at home.

• Set the table, arrange the flowers, and select the serving dishes the day before so on the day of the meal you can attend to the food.

• Clean out your refrigerator and freezer to make room for all those holiday goodies.

GIFTS & GREETINGS

Use this page to make a list of everyone you want to include on your Christmas card list this year. For a personal touch, make beautiful beaded cards like the ones on page 104.

CHRISTMAS CARD LIST

Name	Address	Sent/Received

Gift List

Name	Gift	Sent/Delivered

Thoughtful Gifts for Special Friends

- Make your own personal Christmas cards or stationery using rubber stamps and cardstock. Bundle several cards together and tie with a ribbon to give as a gift.

- Tuck favorite family recipes in a basket with new kitchen linens.

- Record your children singing or playing, and send tapes to relatives who live far away.

- Give someone a gift certificate promising you'll teach them a skill that you do well. If you plan to teach how to embroider, for example, include needles, hoop, fabric, patterns, etc.

- Organize family photos and memorabilia in a scrapbook for a grandparent.

HOLIDAY MEMORIES

Keep a reminder of this holiday's best moments by noting them on these pages.

TREASURED TRADITIONS

Did you add a new twist to a favorite seasonal tradition this year,
or maybe you repeated a familiar routine that gets better every year—
either way, this is a good place to preserve the memory in words.

SPECIAL HOLIDAY EVENTS

List this year's most wonderful happenings on these lines. Make a note of specific
dates if it's something you'd like to do again next year.

Holiday Visits & Visitors

Be sure to recall the highlights of all your Christmas reunions by noting them here.

This Year's Favorite Recipes

Appetizers and Beverages:

Entrées:

Sides and Salads:

Cookies and Candies:

Desserts:

NOTES & IDEAS
FOR NEXT YEAR

THINGS WE LOVED

Use this space to record the best-of-the-best. Whether it's
parties, recipes, gift ideas, or impromptu gatherings, writing it here
will ensure you'll remember it for next holiday season.

WORKS IN PROGRESS

Start now to plan for a terrific Christmas 2004. With your
best ideas written here, you'll be off to a great start.

New Year's Resolutions